OPPORTUNITY INVESTING

How to Revitalize Urban and Rural Communities with Opportunity Funds

BY JIM WHITE, PhD

JLW

Inspiring Excellence
in People

JL White International, LLC
16220 N. Scottsdale Road, Suite 260
Scottsdale, AZ 85254

Note: *The information provided in this book is for informational purposes only and is not intended to be a source of advice with respect to the material presented. The information contained in this book does not constitute legal, financial, or investment advice and should never be used without first consulting with a legal or financial professional to determine what may be best for your individual needs. The publisher and the author and their affiliated entities and individuals do not make any guarantee or other promise as to any results that may be obtained from using the content of this book. You should not make an investment decision without first consulting with your own financial and/or legal advisors and conducting your own research and due diligence. To the maximum extent permitted by law, the publisher and the author and their affiliated entities and individuals disclaim any and all liability in the event any information contained in this book proves to be inaccurate, incomplete, or unreliable, or results in any investment or other losses. Further, the laws and regulations related to the content of this book may vary from state to state and, as of the date of the publication hereof, are still in development on a federal basis.*

978-0-9795216-6-9 Ebook ISBN

978-0-9795216-5-2 Print book ISBN

Printed in the United States of America

I would like to dedicate this book to the 329,709,787 people in the United States who believe we are still the best nation on earth, despite all of our imperfections.

And...with a special dedication to my family who gives so freely of their time and love to support me.

We discover our purpose by uncovering challenges that move our hearts and engage our passions. Purpose is why we get out of bed in the morning. Purpose is what pushes us to the extreme limits of our endurance. Purpose is what makes life worth living and satisfied.

—Jim White, PhD

ACKNOWLEDGMENTS

I would like to express my gratitude to the many people who have contributed to making this book come alive. I especially want to thank the following individuals: Chris Jackson, our General Counsel and COO; Mike Collett, our CPA and researcher; Bill Gheen and Russell Gheen, my fellow board members; Amy Cooper, my book cover designer, researcher, and project manager; Gary M. Krebs, my editor; and so many other talented folks who have been a part of this labor of love.

I also want to thank those individuals and organizations that have allowed me to quote their remarks, as well as to the many people who have spent hours editing and proofreading the work. I would like to thank all of our employees for believing in our vision, mission, and values.

Last but not least, I beg forgiveness of all those who have been with me over the course of years and whose names I have not mentioned.

CONTENTS

INTRODUCTION

Investing—and Living—with Purpose

Let's start by addressing the following obvious question: Why, as a business founder and chairman as well as an investor, do I have such passion for Qualified Opportunity Zones (which we'll refer to as QOZs) and Qualified Opportunity Funds (which we'll refer to as QOFs)?

The answer is simple: I care about people. I care about helping those who have been dealt a bad hand and face economic hardships. I care about improving companies that are struggling. I care about giving new life to distressed communities.

Why am I so interested in helping distressed communities? Because I was raised in one of them myself.

To paraphrase a line I once heard: I was born in Georgia, raised in South Carolina, and grew up in Vietnam. I came from an abusive, low-income rural environment. I began my life in a sharecropper cabin and was a high school dropout. My first job was operating heavy construction machinery. I gained a number of invaluable leadership lessons from having first endured hardships during my childhood and then from having faced such challenging conditions in wartime. These lessons prepared me well for leadership roles down the road.

Throughout my life and career I've had to work my way from the ground up. I had a number of jobs until I was able to pave a lucrative career for myself in a number of corporate areas. I eventually earned three college degrees: a B.S. in Civil Engineering; an MBA; and a Ph.D. in Psychology and Organizational Behavior. With those degrees in place, you can now officially refer to me as "Doc White."

This Doc has spent a lot of time nurturing and tending to companies that had been floundering so they could return to good health. I have devoted over a quarter of a century to coaching, mentoring, and leading individuals to become peak performers while acquiring and running several multi-million dollar companies.

So, now that you know *who* I am, we can return to answering the second question that opened this Introduction. Why do I have such passion for

Qualified Opportunity Zones (QOZs) and Qualified Opportunity Funds (QOFs)?

It all connects back to one central ingredient: *my purpose*.

The most important thing I learned in my life was the answer to the question, "What is my purpose?" Until I was able to pinpoint this, I couldn't resolve any of the other important questions in my life.

People often confuse *purpose* with *reason*. We may work at a specific job simply because we need to make a living. There is nothing wrong with that. We all have to pay our bills.

However, our *purpose* for working should be to *make a life*. Over the years, I've come to know exactly what those three words truly mean and how to apply them to everything I do.

From my earliest memories, I imagined that I was on some kind of mission. I had an implacable unwillingness to allow anything else to interfere with what my destiny was directing me towards. The definition of my purpose has evolved and become clearer over the years. My life's purpose is a never-ending mission.

We all need to find our own individual purpose. I came to clarify mine through a remarkable set of circumstances. It happens I grew up having to deal with pain and hardship. Through a series of chance circumstances and while developing my purpose, I learned how to make the invisible *visible*. I've always had great empathy for the underdog. Using my life path as a guidepost, I sought to identify struggling companies and give them a boost to become high-performing entities. I believed in the people at those companies and the products and/or services they produced. Most importantly, I believed in the communities around these companies that would become improved by my assistance in helping turn them around.

My eyes opened wide when the Tax Cuts and Jobs Act (TCJA) was signed on December 22, 2017. Suddenly, here was a brand new path that fit directly into my purpose. Through Qualified Opportunity Zones (QOZs) and Qualified Opportunity Funds (QOFs), we have a chance to work together to: 1) benefit from the capital gains tax break; 2) make money; and 3) positively impact low-income urban and rural communities and the lives of millions of people. This is a win-win-win for everyone concerned.

In a nutshell, *Opportunity Investing* is about finding and creating opportunities in these QOZs and improving the quality of life for their residents by helping the companies in those areas succeed. If the businesses thrive, the communities will have more jobs and better salaries to offer. More people will want to relocate to these places, which will increase real estate values and breathe new life into local shops and stores. When residents and business owners are doing well, they spend more money on beautifying their homes, storefronts, public buildings, streets, parks, and monuments.

I deeply appreciate your curiosity in learning about how QOFs can help turn these QOZs around, which will restore financial health and pride to these communities. Spread out over dozens, hundreds, and perhaps even thousands of communities, QOFs can help our nation flourish as a whole. Thank you for being part of my life's purpose, which hopefully intersects with yours.

Purpose is out there for everyone who will find his or her way to it. In 1899 politician William Jennings Bryan aptly stated, "Destiny is no matter of chance. It is a matter of choice. It is not a thing to be waited for, it is a thing to be achieved."

Let's achieve a great destiny together.

PART ONE

DEFINING THE PROBLEM

CHAPTER ONE

COMMUNITIES IN DISTRESS

I'm sure I don't need to define the word *distress* for you, but I am going to provide the meaning of it anyway to help paint a picture and put things in context.

In today's language, the word *distress* refers to human suffering, usually due to some type of anxiety, sorrow, or pain. It could be physical, mental, or emotional—or even a combination of one or more of these states.

Alternatively, in business, product inventory may be described as *distressed* when it has depreciated in value. Food products with brief shelf lives (such as fruit, which goes rotten after a few days) and time-sensitive events (such as unsold stadium seats five minutes before the game begins) may both be considered *distressed*.

How Can an Entire Community Be Distressed?

All of the aforementioned meanings aside, there exists another contemporary usage of the word *distress:* one that refers to communities that have fallen into a state of severe socio-economic decline. While there are numerous American cities and towns that are thriving, unfortunately there are also many rural and urban areas across our great nation that have become distressed due to a variety of circumstances and factors.

It is possible, for example, for a stable area to become devastated overnight due to reasons beyond anyone's control. A town or even a major city can become distressed because of a catastrophic event, such as a tornado, hurricane, flood, wildfire, or earthquake. These tragedies can and do happen with all too much frequency, taking a massive toll upon lives, homes, businesses, and entire landscapes. When natural calamities occur, the government is typically called into action to provide emergency assistance and financial relief.

Then there are those distressed rural and urban communities that fall into the category of "man-made" over a short or long-term time frame. The causes of these are often not so simple to explain, especially in areas that at one time were prosperous and flourishing, but fell into sharp decline.

Some communities took major hits during various economic collapses from which they were never able to recover, such as the 2008 recession. Others suffered from political malfeasance or incompetence. Many have been inadvertent casualties of technological progress and humans being replaced by machinery, computers, and digitization. Then there are those companies that believed they could manufacture products and/or perform services better, faster, and cheaper by outsourcing their labor overseas. What was left behind? Destitute cities and towns filled with unemployed people and block-after-block of decaying factories, warehouses, office buildings, and storefronts.

Author Bill Bishop put forth an interesting theory in his book *The Big Sort*. He believes that Americans are not necessarily being divided into political "red states" and "blue states," but rather, are shifting away from poor urban and rural areas to major thriving cities and technological epicenters, such as New York, San Francisco, Los Angeles, Seattle, and Boston. Well-educated people skilled in certain professions have been flocking to places where they believe they can establish high profile career paths, earn top salaries, and live better quality of lives.

No one is blaming anyone for making such a decision, but there is a specific collective ramification. When ambitious and educated people abandon distressed rural and urban communities, they deplete those areas of even more money, talent, and resources.

As a result of so many people and businesses vacating urban and rural communities that are already distressed, the town centers and neighborhoods have become filled with eyesore structures that are constant reminders of the past—good times gone bad. The emotional impact on the citizens of these towns cannot be measured, but one can safely say that "hope" is not a word spoken in abundance, and frustration typically prevails. They do not see a light at the end of the tunnel indicating that their circumstances will ever turn around for the better.

Is America Still the Land of Opportunity?

In my view, the answer to the above question is simple: of course it is. The

United States of America is a powerful country and the quality of life is consistently high for many people. The country's GDP (gross domestic product) is ranked #1 in the world at an estimated $21.5 billion at the time of this writing.

On the other hand, despite our country's vast abundance and wealth, there does exist an obvious financial imbalance. This is not political rhetoric, just a fact: 1% of the population owns 40% of the nation's wealth. America boasts the greatest population of affluent people in the world with 680 billionaires whose wealth totals $3.2 trillion. The nearest country on the list, China, has only 338 billionaires for a total wealth of $1.1 trillion.

Make no mistake: The wealth gap in the United States is the greatest it has seen in half a century. I don't mean to depress you, but, as you'll discover later on in this book, the United States currently has *thousands* of distressed urban and rural communities. They cover the entire breadth of our nation and their populations are diverse. Unfortunately, poverty is a condition that does not discriminate, impacting people of every race, creed, color, gender, and age group, though, as we'll reveal later on in this chapter, it does strike minorities with far greater severity.

In 2018, in spite of a strong GDP and increased Wall Street earnings, the poverty level soared in the United States. One in six people—*46.2 million Americans*—fell below the poverty line that year. It goes without saying that the highest percentage of impoverished people resides in distressed communities. According to the "2018 Distressed Communities Index" released by the Economic Innovation Group (EIG) in October of that year, approximately 86.5 million Americans live in prosperous zip codes, whereas 50 million Americans reside in ones that are distressed.

So, Who Are Prospering?

First, let's review the good news: Where are America's most "elite" communities?

If one were to take a potshot guess at which cities have the most prosperous zip codes in the country, you might propose New York, Los Angeles, or Chicago. Surprise—not one of these even makes the top ten. In fact, as we'll later explore, Chicago has its own unique problems, starting with infrastructure.

The only major city that automatically leaps to mind and appears on the list? San Francisco.

Interestingly, three states—Arizona (three cities), California (three cities), and Texas (two cities)—comprise most of the top ten. The number one and number two slots are held by cities most northerners have probably never even heard of: Gilbert, Arizona and Plano, Texas.

Gilbert, Arizona is a unique case study. The city, which has a population of around 231,000, is located in the southeast valley of the Phoenix metropolitan area. A whopping 99% of its population resides in prosperous zip codes. Businesses and investors are drawn to Gilbert in the following key industries:

- **Life Sciences:** known for health care facilities and cutting-edge stem cell research.

- **Clean Technology and Renewable Energy:** the Quality Jobs Through Renewable Industries Program has generated an influx of capital investment money and thousands of new jobs.

- **Aerospace and Aviation:** more than 1,200 aerospace and defense companies contribute nearly $15 billion annually and sustain 150,000+ jobs.

- **Manufacturing:** provides nearly 50,000 jobs.

- **Advanced Business Services:** 41% of the city has a bachelor's degree or higher. The city employs specialists in accounting, financial analysis, law, design, marketing, insurance, architecture, engineering, venture capital, investment banking, real estate, and data centers.

All of this is wonderful news for the thriving Gilbert business and family community. The above list of key industries makes it abundantly clear that executives, investors, leaders, and citizens care deeply about the community and have a great deal of pride in its number one status. In fact, as the city experiences its centennial in 2020, the leadership of the community recognizes that conditions and circumstances can change in a hurry. This is why they refuse to rest on their laurels, leave things to chance, or do anything that might risk losing their status. Having witnessed and studied the rapid declines of several neighboring areas that reverted from prosperous to a state of distress, they refuse to allow anything to slip.

Dubbing Gilbert "the City of the Future" for their anniversary, the leaders are doubling down on maintaining a strong economy, a prosperous community, and an exceptionally built environment. They are focusing on keeping the city's aging infrastructure up-to-date, building an educated workforce, and integrating innovation into all areas of business.

In other words, Gilbert is fully *invested* in its community.

The Shocking Truth

Now we get to the nitty-gritty: the areas in America with the most distressed zip codes. This list is revealing in how it is more spread out across the continent; only one state, Ohio, appears twice. Unlike the list of most prosperous cities, the majority of these are well known and almost all of them had heydays at one time or another:

1. Cleveland, Ohio.
2. Newark, New Jersey.
3. Buffalo, New York.
4. Detroit, Michigan.
5. Toledo, Ohio.
6. Memphis, Tennessee.
7. Milwaukee, Wisconsin.
8. Stockton, California.
9. Philadelphia, Pennsylvania.
10. Tucson, Arizona.

Let's take a closer look at number nine on the list: Philadelphia (population 1.6 million, 49.3% of which is in distressed zip codes). One of our original magnificent colonial cities and the largest one at the time, Philadelphia was the birthplace of both the Constitution and the Declaration of Independence. The city lays claim to many remarkable firsts in our nation's history: the first hospital (Philadelphia Hospital, co-founded by Benjamin Franklin in 1751); the first daily newspaper (*Philadelphia Packet and Daily Advertiser*, 1784); the first university (University of Pennsylvania, 1749); and the first zoo (Philadelphia Zoo, 1874). Today, Philadelphia is home to our precious Liberty Bell and the city's staple culinary contribution, the Philly Cheesesteak.

By all accounts, this great city should rank among those with the *highest* quality of life in America and serve as a magnet for luring in businesses and families. Unfortunately, the economic situation in Philadelphia is far from being on par with its patriotic history. When many people envision the city, they think of the slummy streets depicted in the *Rocky* films, not the stately historic sites situated in Independence National Historical Park (where more than two dozen landmarks, such as the Liberty Bell and Independence Hall, may be visited).

Five Major Distressed Cities Not Among the Top Ten

Scrolling further down the list of distressed cities after the top ten, one encounters several other eye-opening metropolitan zip codes that at one time were American hubs: St. Louis, MO; Baltimore, MD; Hartford, CT; and Chicago-Elgin-Aurora, IL. The struggling economic status of these former powerhouses is largely due to extreme population reductions.

- **St. Louis, MO:** This historic city saw its metropolitan population decline by 1.1% to 2.8 million residents, making it the city that suffered the steepest dip in 2018. According to the U.S. Census, approximately one out of four residents live in poverty. The median household income is less than $36,000, which is well below the national figure.

- **Baltimore, MD:** The Baltimore metropolitan area also declined by 1.1% to 2.8 million residents. The core city's population shrank to a one hundred-year low, reversing a push from Mayor Stephanie Rawlings-Blake to attract 10,000 new families to Baltimore. Some residents are moving amidst a rising crime rate and budget issues.

- **Hartford, CT:** The Hartford, Connecticut region saw its population shrink by 0.5% to 1.2 million people in 2018. Hartford was ranked as one of the fifty worst cities in the country by 24/7 Wall St. Its 6.6% unemployment rate is higher than the national rate of 4.9%. The crime rate is more than double the national average (938 violent crimes for every 100,000 city residents in 2016 versus the national crime ratio of 386 per 100,000 people).

- **Chicago-Elgin-Aurora, IL:** The population in the Chicago metropolitan area declined by 0.3% to 9.5 million people. The harsh weather isn't the only factor in the exodus; Chicagoans face high taxes, soaring crime rates, and struggling infrastructure. (You'll find more about this later in the chapter.)

The Glass Half Full

Not all of the news on the list of most distressed cities is bad. Stockton, CA (population 300,000; 69.8% population in distressed zip codes)—which is situated in an agricultural area eighty miles northeast of San Jose—has actually been improving the past several years, although it did make the top ten list of distressed cities. Having filed bankruptcy in 2013, the city has made a remarkable, if imperfect, financial turnaround and at least now has the means to pay its bills. Housing is up and neighborhoods are being repaired. The main continuing challenges are that the city is struggling to sustain the high cost of its pensions, and its infrastructure is aging.

Cities such as Stockton and thousands of others like it require constant attention and TLC. When politicians, businesspeople, and leading citizens fail to support their communities and make them appealing for businesses and investors, their neighborhoods crumble and the quality of life suffers for everyone.

What Is Happening in Distressed Communities?

While every rural and urban community is unique, there are several common themes that have caused the population declines and financial struggles in these areas. In virtually all instances, minority groups (i.e., all ethnic groups excluding non-Hispanic white) continue to take the greatest financial hit when neighborhoods become distressed.

Additionally, community infrastructure suffers, which harms the quality of life and safety of the population, discourages businesses, and negates tourism. While the infrastructure focus and labeling of each category can vary depending on the needs of the region, it generally covers these core areas: transportation (such as bus and subway systems); energy (such as electrical grids); water (such as clean tap water); public safety (such as alerts and protections against environmental disasters, i.e., floods); health (such as hospitals); education (such as schools); and public spaces (such as parks and beaches).

Areas infested with drugs and crime often become distressed. The reverse is also true: Communities that become distressed fall prey to a greater volume of drugs and crime. It goes without saying that good folks don't want to live in places that are unsafe for their families. Similarly, startup businesses become scared off by areas with high crime rates and choose not to set up shop there.

When people and businesses abandon a city, the economies plummet. The area becomes an unappealing place to live and work; people choose not to relocate there, while businesses place their factories, office spaces, and resources in safer havens. All of these factors damage the reputation of a community and form a disastrous circular pattern that becomes seemingly impossible to reverse.

Minorities Are Suffering the Most

Despite modest progress towards inclusion, America has a long way to go in terms of how minorities fare in our communities. The imbalance remains a major concern in rural and urban areas throughout our country. Minorities represent **56%** of the population in distressed communities, yet such groups comprise only 38% of the national population.

The contrast becomes even more pronounced when considering the fact that non-Hispanic white people account for nearly *three-quarters* of the populations in prosperous zip codes. A nation in which all people are born with the right to be treated as equals should not have gaps like this or be divided culturally into resulting unintentionally segregated areas of "haves" and "have nots."

Infrastructure Has Fallen Apart

There are, unfortunately, thousands of instances of how failing infrastructure wreaks havoc on distressed communities. Naturally, if communities become distressed, they don't have the funds to do what is necessary to keep things running smoothly and efficiently while establishing the groundwork for making their environments clean, safe, and attractive. Infrastructure often means maintaining, protecting, and preserving the history of a community, which can take the form of objects (such as monuments and park benches), buildings (such as historic landmarks), and public events (such as celebrations of its accomplished citizens and famous battles that occurred there).

Without proper infrastructure, a community and its legacy can deteriorate. Sometimes it impacts the "visual appeal" of the area—the condition of public buildings and parks—but other times the result cuts to the bone by reducing the quality of education for the children and risking the safety of residents, workers, and visitors.

Let's take a closer look at a few examples.

In February 2017, the Oroville Dam spillway, located in Oroville, CA, became severely damaged and necessitated the evacuation of more than 180,000 people. One cause of the disaster was that the area had rapidly transformed from a period of drought to an inundation of snow and rainwater, which collected in the dam. As it turns out, the calamity could have been prevented if the money and resources had been made available when the problems were first identified. In 2005, environmental groups issued warnings to the federal government in advance and requested funds to repair the dam before it was too late. The proposal was rejected. The cost of repairing the dam and cleaning up the damaged community far exceeded what would have been required to solidify the dam back in 2005.

Oroville is far from alone in terms of infrastructure challenges. The American Society of Civil Engineers recently gave the country a "D" grade for its maintenance of dams. This is most disconcerting when you consider that the average age of America's dams is fifty-six years. If we don't prioritize infrastructure, more calamities may be on the way. Meanwhile, Oroville, CA and its population of 19,000 citizens paid a steep price for the neglect; it is listed as a distressed community and has teetered on the brink of bankruptcy.

Many of us take our drinking water for granted, and we don't give a second thought to the age of the pipes the water travels through. The fact is, America's water pipes are corroding, leaking, and bursting at a frightful rate. The average age of our country's water pipes is forty-five at the time this book is being published. There are some 600 towns and counties that have cast iron water pipes over a century old that have never been replaced.

Numerous American QOZ areas, such as in Flint, Michigan and Compton, California do not have safe drinking water. The infrastructure problems have long since been identified, but the communities simply don't have the funds to subsidize necessary repairs and upgrades.

As if Detroit, MI doesn't have enough to worry about with high unemployment (currently at 8.8% vs. 3.6% national average) and the second highest crime rate (2,057 incidents per 100,000 residents and 267 murders in 2017), its infrastructure is in a state of decline and disarray. On January 2019, a water main break disrupted the annual North American International Auto Show—a major event for this area, to say the least, despite flagging attendance from carmakers—causing a "boil water" advisory due to unsafe drinking water. In February 2019, a group of beleaguered residents had to sue the city's Water and Sewerage Department for a drainage fee (which they labeled a "tax") to pay for the community's aging storm water infrastructure.

It is terrifying to think about the possibility of any major bridge structure collapsing—but that is a genuine possibility in the six-county Chicago metro area. Over 400 bridges (12% of the total) have been dubbed "structurally deficient" by inspectors. If much-needed repairs on the structures and decks of these bridges aren't subsidized, people's lives will continue to be at great risk.

Drugs and Crime

In February 2019, 24/7 Wall St. named the twenty-five most dangerous cities in America. It's no coincidence that all of them are also distressed areas; drugs and crime tend to go hand-in-hand with economic insolvency.

Earlier in this chapter I pointed out several major cities that have become distressed and continue to face population declines. One such city, St. Louis, MO, also had the dubious honor of being ranked by the FBI as "the most dangerous city in America" in 2017. While this particular FBI report also considers natural disasters (such as earthquakes, flooding, hail, hurricanes, and tornadoes) as part of the overall criteria for "dangerous," the crime rate that year soared 8.8% and over two hundred people were murdered. All of this occurred in spite of the fact that St. Louis has the largest police force per capita.

Meanwhile, Cincinnati, OH topped the list of cities suffering from the worst drug problems. More than one quarter of the city's population lives in poverty. Communities in Cincinnati are witnessing an inordinately high rate of drug overdoses, which increased 1,000% over a five-year span due to users' recently adopted practice of combining synthetic opioids like fentanyl and carfentanil with common street drugs like cocaine.

This entire book could be devoted to the harsh realities of the opioid crisis and its impact on American cities. One simple fact from January 2019 stands out: *130 lives are claimed every single day in our country by opioid addiction.*

Baltimore, MD—along with many other great American cities—has been plagued by the opioid crisis. In addition to suffering from rising crime rates, gun violence, and government corruption, Baltimore witnessed a shocking 692 opioid-related deaths in 2017—the highest in the United States. The city struggles to provide adequate treatment and medication for those coping with opioid addiction, especially minorities.

Businesses Must Take Some Responsibility

You've gathered by now that our distressed urban and rural communities are facing dire situations in a number of different areas. Like the chicken and the egg, it doesn't matter which came first—the poverty, the collapsed infrastructure, or the drugs/crime scaring businesses into retreating. The results are still the same with minorities bearing the brunt of the fallout. Without businesses investing in communities, everything collapses one-by-one like a series of Dominoes.

In my view, there shouldn't be any politics involved in outsourcing. Keeping as many jobs as possible on American soil should be a primary responsibility of every corporate executive and business owner. Politicians on all sides of the equation make promises such as tax breaks that never seem to do the trick in terms of retaining workforces or bringing them back once they're gone. The bottom-line usually wins out: Companies inevitably go with the cheapest possible option.

In 2017, Carrier, a producer of air conditioners, shipped hundreds of jobs from Indiana to Mexico only one year after President Trump claimed to have saved them. Most people don't realize that Carrier's parent company, United Technologies, had already sent 5,000 jobs overseas over a span of two decades, despite having received billions of dollars in government contracts.

This is by no means a unique circumstance. Fortune 500 companies in a range of Industries have been outsourcing their labor: Morgan Stanley, IBM, GE, AT&T, and Microsoft, to name a few. If the business titans don't lead by example and keep jobs in the United States, why should others be encouraged to follow?

Outsourcing to another country is not the only issue. When choosing locations for their headquarters, factories, and warehouses in the United States, major companies tend to select the healthiest, most prosperous areas without giving much consideration to moving into struggling communities that might benefit from their support.

Perhaps the most famous public example of a company wielding its massive power occurred when Amazon deliberated on the location of its new headquarters. Not only was Amazon intending to go the logical, predictable route of searching for an area with the biggest incentives (i.e., tax breaks), it expressed preferences for: a metropolitan area with more than one million people; a stable and business-friendly environment; an urban or suburban location with the potential to attract and retain strong technical talent; and a community that thinks "big and creatively."

Perhaps Amazon could apply the words "big and creatively" to its own search criteria. Imagine what might happen if a juggernaut like Amazon were to instead think counter-intuitively and move its workforce to a *distressed area in America*? There are some obvious risks—especially if drugs and crime are already prevalent—but right away property and labor costs would be lower for them because the area is already on the downside. The business could reassign the money saved on those items to invest in the surrounding communities. With the job and population increases and the potential for a turnaround on the horizon from such support, more businesses—real estate agencies, restaurants, and hotels—would enter the area to fill increasing needs. Suddenly, the citizens would see what is happening and feel optimistic. Once again they take pride in their community and initiate beautifying projects to make it better.

Ultimately, Amazon received some *238 proposals*, including from Washington, D.C., New York, Boston, Austin, and Portland—all filled with many flourishing zip codes. The company came to terms with Queens, New York for a location, but then bowed out when politicians, labor leaders, and local storeowners rallied against the $3 billion in state and city tax breaks Amazon would have garnered.

It is evident that Amazon never had any intention of establishing its headquarters anywhere other than in an area that was already prosperous, instead of taking the opportunity to improve a distressed community. In essence, they dangled the carrot to stir controversy and inflate bids. As *The New Republic* stated: "…it's clear now that the company never intended to save a struggling American city, transforming its economy, infrastructure, and perhaps even schools; it only ever made sense, in purely capitalist terms, to choose a city that already was flourishing. The dozens of desperate bidders, from Detroit to Stonecrest, were nothing but pawns in a rigged, zero-sum game they've been losing for decades."

If a company such as Amazon—which has substantial financial means—doesn't take the lead when choosing a location, who else is going to set the example? Why would smaller businesses attempt to accomplish something that a powerhouse like Amazon wouldn't even consider?

In the next chapter, we'll examine the job market in distressed urban and rural areas in greater detail. We will also gain a greater understanding of why it doesn't work when only a handful of metropolitan areas produce as many jobs as the rest of the nation combined.

CHAPTER TWO

THE PLAIN FACTS ABOUT AMERICA'S DISTRESSED URBAN AND RURAL AREAS

The first national census of the United States was conducted on August 2, 1790 on what was then known as "Census Day." At the time, the newly founded country had a population of just below four million people.

Over a century later, on July 1, 1902, the United States Census Bureau was formed to oversee the entire process of calculating the country's demographics. The census at that time (taken two years earlier, in 1900) reported a population of slightly above 76.2 million.

The most recent United States Census, taken in 2010, reported 308.7 million Americans. Currently, the Census Bureau estimates the American population consists of nearly 330 million people.

My, we have grown a lot since the founding of our nation! That is a lot of people to employ, care for, and protect. In terms of population, we are the third largest nation in the world, although a far distance behind China (1.42 billion people) and India (1.369 billion people).

Today, the United States Census Bureau, which is part of the United States Department of Commerce, conducts an official decennial (meaning: every ten years) national census. The 2010 census may seem like an eternity ago—and we have to wait until the unveiling of the 2020 results for the next one—but keep in mind that data collection is a major national endeavor and a great deal is riding upon making sure it is as accurate as possible. The good news is that additional data is estimated and assessed on a regular basis by the United States Census Bureau between census rollouts, as reported on their website at **https://www.census.gov**.

You may by wondering: Why is all of this background on the census so important to impart in this book? The answer is simple: Census data is the foremost determination of our nation's overall size, financial health, and general wellbeing. Think of it like a socio-economic check-up. Not only does it reveal an enormous amount of critical facts about the American people, it serves as the leading provider of information about where our population resides and where the jobs, businesses, and money are situated.

Many long-term socio-economic conclusions end up being drawn from this massive data bank and, once it's all collected, other divisions of the government (such as the United States Department of the Treasury) make important decisions about how supportive measures and funds are allocated based on financial need. The census culls data about population, age, sex, ethnicity, race and Hispanic origin, housing arrangements, health, the labor force, household income, veterans, types of businesses, and many other areas to help reflect the current state of our country and residents.

The census, therefore, is the main driver behind how distressed areas are identified and then assigned as Qualified Opportunity Zones (QOZs), which we will cover in detail in Part Two.

All of the surveyed, assembled, and disseminated data means several things with regard to our purpose in understanding the following:

- Our nation's health.

- What the job market looks like.

- How businesses located in struggling rural and urban areas are faring.

- Why we all shouldn't be following the kicked soccer ball.

In this chapter, we'll probe deeper into each of the aforementioned issues with the objective of visualizing a clear picture of the unfortunate socio-economic inequalities that exist in America's communities.

Not Living Longer and Not Prospering

People commonly believe that Americans have a better quality of life today than those who lived a century ago. We presume that modern medicine is helping us enjoy longer life expectancies and sustain better health into our old age than past generations. This is mostly true, as confirmed by one data point: The median age of United States citizens is thirty-eight years of age, compared with 29.5 in 1960.

It won't surprise you to read that the average American lifespan steadily increased year-after-year, up right until 2015. But now you are in for some shocking news: After decades of lifespan improvement, the average American lifespan *declined* two years in a row, in 2016 and 2017 respectively, and is now around 78.7. The United States is heading in the reverse and dying younger, whereas well over a dozen countries including Japan (84.1 years), Switzerland (83.7), and Australia (82.5) are far outliving us.

Hold on for just one second. Those facts are head-scratchers! With all of the amazing advances in science and medicine happening in our great country—not to mention our vast wealth and resources—how can lifespans suddenly be *decreasing*?

Science and medicine are not to blame. To be sure, cancer-related deaths have been steadily dropping due to reduced smoking, early disease detection, and improved cancer treatments. Deaths due to heart attack declined 14.6% between 2006 and 2016.

So, what is the cause of our deteriorating lifespan? It comes down to the unfolding tragedy identified in the previous chapter: drug addiction-related overdoses and suicides, especially among younger people. Deaths due to opioid addiction and other drugs increased *137%* between 2000 and 2014. The trend only seems to be worsening: As mentioned earlier, *130 lives are claimed every single day in our country by opioid addiction.*

The related national suicide rate has shot up to 24% between 1999 and 2014.

Another way of putting it is that America's addiction crisis is accelerating at a much greater rate than the success rates in science and medicine, at least in terms of keeping us alive. And, since the opioid crisis has hit distressed areas much harder than prosperous ones, those folks are at a significantly higher risk of overdoses and suicides.

It's All About Where the Jobs Are

As of this writing, the unemployment rate in the United States is declining. Currently, 5.8 million people are unemployed, or 3.6%, which is the lowest it's been since December 1969. This is a wonderful trend that we all hope continues.

Questions: *Shouldn't we be celebrating? With such strong employment news, what's the problem?*

Answer: *This is yet another unfortunate instance of "haves" vs. "have nots."*

The fact is, although numerous areas across the country suffered from job losses during the 2007-2008 recession, the prosperous ones were able to recoup those losses over time; many even managed to come out well ahead. Meanwhile, the distressed areas have failed to recover from the recession and largely *continue* to decline; predictions indicate that most will never improve.

The numbers speak for themselves: In 2016, prosperous zip codes employed 3.6 million more people than they did in 2007. Meanwhile, during that same time frame, distressed zip codes *lost* 1.4 million jobs.

As I stated, the nation's overall low unemployment rate is a wonderful thing—but not when such a tremendous imbalance has been festering. In the previous chapter, I pointed out the record-breaking wealth gap in the country and how this hurts minorities far more than non-minorities.

How can we fully embrace this low unemployment rate when so many people in distressed communities are struggling worse than ever?

It's Not "Just Business"

Naturally, the statistics on businesses tell a story that is similar to the unemployment rates. Between 2012-2016, 180,000 new businesses were gained in prosperous zip codes. By contrast, in that same time frame, 13,300 businesses were shuttered in distressed zip codes. As the Economic Innovation Group reported in the 2018 Communities Index, "Prosperous zip codes added more business establishments during the recovery years than the bottom 80 percent of zip codes combined."

While we would like to think that everything gradually "returned to normal" for American businesses after the 2007-2008 recession, this was only true in select areas. On the one hand, there were nearly 53,000 more businesses in the U.S. between the years spanning the end of the recession and 2016. On the other hand, the combined total of just five metro counties—Los Angeles, CA; Brooklyn, NY; Harris, TX (Houston); Queens, NY; and Miami-Dade, FL—exceeded the national number with 55,000 more businesses in that same time frame.

On the surface this seems completely illogical: How can five counties have a higher increase in the number of businesses than the entire country? And yet, the facts tell the story. The five aforementioned counties were business magnets, whereas many other areas throughout the nation were losing companies and bleeding employment numbers. Without Los Angeles, Brooklyn, Harris, Queens, and Miami-Dade, the nation's economic picture would, in fact, start to look somewhat bleak.

If a client, customer, business partner, or competitor were to say to you the cliché "It's just business," you know it actually means "Nothing personal, I just ripped you off for the money." In these instances, the expression is said with a knowing smirk, as if it's understood that everyone is out for him or herself and therefore such behavior is perfectly excusable.

When it comes to business decisions (such as factory location) ending up being purely about financial criteria (such as tax benefits), it's as if those companies are telling struggling parts of the country: "It's okay that I just ripped you off and am heading to a better city than yours—*it's just business.*"

But it's *not* okay—and it's *not* "just business." I do not wish anything negative to happen anywhere, but just imagine for a moment if something catastrophic were to occur, impacting our thriving areas. Our country would be in dire straits, for sure, since there wouldn't be other areas capable of taking up the slack.

To cite another unfortunate cliché, we already have way too many golden eggs in just a few baskets and, for the health and long-term stability of our nation, we must spread our business ventures out wider and be more inclusive to distressed urban and rural areas that are desperately in need of a boost.

Everyone Is Following the Soccer Ball

According to *Inc.* magazine, the best places to start a business are in the following cities: Austin, Salt Lake City, Raleigh, Nashville, San Francisco, San Jose, San Diego, Denver, Orlando, and Portland. These cities were ranked according to the following favorable criteria:

- Rate of Entrepreneurship.

- High Growth Company Density.

- Population Density.

- Net Business Creation.

- Wage Growth.

- Job Creation.

- Early-Stage Funding Deals.

In other words, like toddlers playing soccer, the ball gets kicked and a dozen kids race at exactly the same time to get to it first. Some kids elbow each other; some trip over each other; and the rest lag behind and eventually give up, counting the number of weeds on the ground. Meanwhile, no one is defending the goalpost, which is left virtually unguarded. The poor goalie is left standing there all alone, helpless for when the swarm comes charging back her way and kicks the ball over her head into the net.

Please do not misunderstand: I'm not disparaging *Inc.* or any of the fine cities cited above. *Inc.* is providing a valuable service to its readership. The top ten cities they cite are truly wonderful places to live, work, and start a business, and I would never discourage anyone from living or working in any of them.

What about all of the places that are being abandoned for these brighter horizons? Who is supporting and investing in them? How will they ever stand a chance of improving if the soccer ball keeps getting kicked in the same direction over and over? Essentially, the team that has the fastest and strongest kids claiming the ball will score every goal and win every game.

Instead, just imagine for one moment what might happen if distressed areas such as Milwaukee, Buffalo, Cleveland, Philadelphia, Toledo, Memphis, Stockton, and Detroit were to receive a thumbs-up recommendation as places to start a business because they were among the *worst places* to do so? Might that help spread the wealth, improve those communities, and strengthen our nation as a whole?

Yes, I am well aware of the inherent risks in betting against the odds and supporting the underdog. This is precisely where Qualified Opportunity Funds and Qualified Opportunity Zones enter the picture.

As you'll discover in Part Two, we now have a solution that alleviates those risks while enabling investors, entrepreneurs, and business owners to simultaneously garner short- and long-term profit. As a bonus, new life is breathed into these communities with job creation, population increases, and an excited customer base. Ultimately, we all feel a sense of pride because we are working together to help our neighbors and strengthen our nation as a whole.

Isn't that what the United States of America is all about?

PART TWO

DEVELOPING THE SOLUTION

CHAPTER THREE

WHAT IS THE TAX CUTS AND JOBS ACT (TCJA) OF 2017?

On December 22, 2017, President Donald J. Trump signed the $1.5 trillion Tax Cuts and Jobs Act (TCJA) into law. It was the most exhaustive tax law legislation approved since the Internal Revenue Code of 1986.

Reactions to the bill were split along party lines. It was proposed by Republicans, and all senators from that party except one (Bob Corker) voted "yea." Every single Democrat voted against the bill, as did two Independents. The final tally was 51-49 "yeas" vs. "nays," which enabled it to proceed up the chain for presidential signature.

The President and Republicans hailed it as an unbridled success. According to the Tax Foundation—the nation's leading independent tax policy nonprofit—the bill effectively made improvements in tax law, including simplifying the process and reducing the taxes for 80% of Americans. The Foundation also believes it will raise the national GDP (gross domestic product) by 1.7% and increase wages by 1.5%. The standard tax deduction for individuals and couples doubled to $12,000 and $24,000, respectively. On the other hand, TCJA also limits various key deductions, such as the mortgage interest deduction and state and local taxes paid deductions.

Not everyone agreed with the intent behind the bill or the above findings. The debates and controversies took place before, during, and after the legislation was approved. Democrats expressed immense frustration, stating that the bill was stuffed down everyone's throats without enough time for the document to be fully reviewed by the individuals voting on it—especially when it had gone through several rounds of changes and people didn't even know what ended up in the final version. Senators Chuck Schumer (New

York), Elizabeth Warren (Massachusetts), and Cory Booker (New Jersey) were particularly outspoken against the bill, as were noted economists Paul Krugman (*New York Times* columnist and Nobel Prize winner) and Richard Thaler (distinguished professor and Nobel Prize winner). Krugman went as far as calling it "The biggest scam in history."

Billionaire investor Warren Buffett, who stood to make millions in additional profits from the tax cuts, didn't hesitate to volunteer, "I don't think I need a tax cut." With regard to changes in the death tax he reflected, "I sure don't think it's good for a society where there's a ton of inequality…"

Take a Bad Bill and Make It Better

We don't need to go into the weeds about all of the politics involved. I won't speak to whether or not I agree or disagree with Republicans, the long-term assessment from the Tax Foundation, or the objections from the Democrats. Only time will tell which point of view is correct and even then it is for others to interpret the results and determine who was on the right side of history.

However, the aforementioned potential outcomes aside, the Tax Cuts and Jobs Act of 2017 is without a doubt disproportionately favorable to the wealthiest Americans, and therefore what I would consider to be a "bad bill." The slightly paraphrased lesson of The Beatles' song "Hey Jude" in the above heading can be applied in this instance. The bill most certainly isn't *all bad* and *can be made much better*. In fact, if investors, venture capitalists, entrepreneurs, and state legislators pay attention to certain aspects of the tax bill, it could pay off richly for designated distressed areas that fit the criteria (which we will review in depth; stay tuned in later chapters)—as well as for the investment community.

How will all of this be made possible? All one needs to do is flip to page 130 of the tax bill, where Qualified Opportunity Zones (QOZs) are included in the bill with the intent of improving distressed communities that have been impacted by issues described in Part One of this book: population declines, poverty, drugs, crime, infrastructure, and more.

Make no mistake: This is a truly remarkable inclusion that Republicans, Democrats, and Independents alike should all join together to celebrate.

But how did this unlikely provision find its way into the tax bill? Let's start peeling the onion to examine what is underneath all of those layers.

The Backstory

The idea behind QOZs was first outlined in April 2015 in a paper entitled "Unlocking Private Capital to Facilitate Economic Growth in Distressed Areas," by Jared Bernstein and Kevin Hassett, chairs of a Washington-based think tank known as the Economic Innovation Group (EIG), which is subsidized by tech mogul Sean Parker. The thesis of the article was a proposal to reduce the impact "of the uneven economic recovery through geographically focused economic policies designed to counteract poverty with special incentives to private investors."

The aforementioned report caught the attention of Republican South Carolina Senator Tim Scott. The African-American politician grew up in a poor area of North Charleston and was raised by his single mom, who worked sixteen-hour shifts as a nursing assistant to make ends meet. Inspired by his mentor, a local Chick-fil-A owner named John Moniz, Scott finished college and eventually became a Republican businessman and politician. A certain South Carolina governor, Nikki Haley (later U.S. ambassador to the United Nations 2017-2018), named him as the mid-term replacement for retiring Senator Jim DeMint. Scott won his first full-term election in 2016.

Dedicated to fighting economic hardship and unemployment, Senator Scott proposed various Opportunity Fund bills; they were bipartisan and even included Democratic New Jersey Senator Cory Booker as a co-sponsor. Scott introduced the idea of QOZs to President Trump who was supportive, and ultimately it became part of the Tax Cuts and Jobs Act of 2017.

In Subchapter Z of the TCJA, the rules, regulations, and benefits of QOZs are all laid out in granular detail, although it requires a great deal of unpacking and explanation to interpret. The cost of this program was a half billion dollars, a mere fraction of the overall $1 trillion tax plan.

This all sounds wonderful, right? It would be—except for the fact that not enough people pay attention to Subchapter Z of the TCJA. As a result, QOZs tend to fall under the radar. Amidst all of the smoke from raging political fires, Republican politicians—aside from Senator Scott—hardly ever mention them. The majority of Democrats are mistrustful of QOZs because they are associated with a bill they despise, are part of legislation created by the opposing party and presidential administration, and/or they simply don't know enough about them or understand what they can accomplish.

No matter the reason, too many eyes are glazing over this important piece of legislation. Even politicians who loathe the tax bill must look past politics and prop up QOZs as a major positive outcome of the Tax Cuts and Jobs Act of 2017. QOZs and QOFs have the potential to benefit many people in a wide variety of ways.

In other words, let's *take a bad bill and make it better.*

Opportunity Knocks

Although Subchapter Z is perhaps the least known and most underappreciated section of the TCJA, it is a rare piece of legislation that encourages investing in areas that can achieve tax savings and help the greater good. It incentivizes private investors to accomplish what our government has been unable to do for years to improve low-income urban and rural areas that fit the criteria.

We will explore the TCJA in complete detail in Chapter Four with regard to defining QOZs and laying the specific groundwork for everything you can do in those areas. For now, what you need to know is that you have a golden opportunity to connect your head and heart with your wallet and change numerous lives in a positive way.

If we wave the flag and rally behind QOZs and QOFs, our distressed rural and urban communities have an opportunity to rise out of low-income status, which means more business and job opportunities will be available for the millions of people who live in these approved zones. (Hang in there—you'll find out the staggering number in the next chapter.) The wealth will be spread out much further than in just a handful of areas, which makes our economy and nation as a whole even healthier and more powerful.

Thanks to the efforts of the Economic Innovation Group, Senator Tim Scott, Senator Cory Booker, and a few other politicians, our government is committed to legislation that is locked in place until 2048. This provides ample time for all of us to work together to turn those economically distressed QOZ locations around. However, as you will learn in later chapters, the potential tax savings diminish the longer one waits to invest—so you need to start paying attention right this minute and get straight to work.

Is it sexy to start a business in these areas? Not in the least.

Will *Inc.*, *Fortune*, *The Wall Street Journal*, and all the rest recommend investing in QOZ areas in their annual roundups? Highly unlikely—but none of that matters a single bit.

Whether you are a venture capitalist, fund manager, investor, entrepreneur, or elected official, listen up! Here is your chance to change the status quo by funneling capital into the communities that need it most and create a win-win situation for everyone.

Opportunity is knocking: Let's open the door and invite it inside.

CHAPTER FOUR

WHAT IS A QUALIFIED OPPORTUNITY ZONE (QOZ)?

You now know that the Tax Cuts and Jobs Act (TCJA) of 2017 provides a provision called Qualified Opportunity Zones (QOZs) that incentivizes investors to devote their money and resources in approved distressed areas. (The key word here, as you will discover, is the word *approved*.) The designation of QOZs remains in effect until 2028.

But *what is a QOZ* and *how does a community qualify as one*? Let's dig into the TCJA and provide some answers to these two all-important questions.

One crucial point for you to understand as you follow the explanations: *Not all distressed areas qualify as QOZs according to the government criteria.* There may be quite a few that miss the mark for one reason or another. It is possible for a distressed community to fail to qualify, even though it is situated in close proximity to a QOZ. Sometimes the reasons why are not so clear-cut. It could be as simple as the government official failing to properly nominate the area, which, as you'll discover, is an essential part of the process.

As a result of the above, the delineations between "distressed community" and "distressed community that qualifies as a QOZ" were occasionally challenging even for this author to figure out during the process of researching and writing this book. But don't worry: We will make 100% certain you avoid potential pitfalls and confusion.

With that disclaimer out of the way, we are going to make understanding QOZs and related terminology as super simple to understand as possible: Just follow the alphabet.

The ABCs of QOZs

As one might expect, the tax bill is not easy reading. I'll do my best to break down the relevant parts and simplify them. I call this "the ABCs of QOZs."

In the next few sections, we will cover:

- **A** = Government definition of *QOZs.*

- **B** = Government definition of *low-income community.*

- **C** = Government rules on *how* QOZs are nominated and *who* approves them.

A: Government Definition of QOZs

On page 130 Subchapter Z section (A) of the tax bill, a QOZ is defined exactly as stated below:

> *(a) QUALIFIED OPPORTUNITY ZONE DEFINED.—For the purposes of this subchapter, the term 'qualified opportunity zone' means a population census tract that is a low-income community that is designated as a qualified opportunity zone.*

What does all of the above legal gobbledygook mean? Allow me to translate it into English. First, you need to know that a *population census tract* is defined as a neighborhood identified by the United States Census Bureau (remember this government department discussed at length back in Chapter Two?) for analyzing the resident populations. Typically, a population census tract consists of 2,500-8,000 people.

A Qualified Census Tract (QCT) is any census tract (or equivalent geographic area defined by the Census Bureau) in which at least 50% of households have an income less than 60% of the Area Median Gross Income (AMGI).

B: Government Definition of a Low-Income Community

The TCJA contains a lot of subchapters and subsections with various letters and strange numbers, but let's ignore all of them to hone in on the letter *B* of our ABCs in order to interpret the phrase *low-income community.*

> *(b) DESIGNATION.—*

(1) IN GENERAL.—For purposes of subsection (A), a population cen-sus tract that is a low-income community is designated as a qualified opportunity zone if—

Let's pause right there. This passage requires some explanation, espe-cially since the document later references U.S. Internal Revenue Code 45D(e), in which a community is categorized as *low-income* if it fulfills the following conditions:

- The poverty for such a tract is at least 20%.

- *Or:* In the case of a tract not located within a metropolitan area, the median income for the area does not exceed 80% of the state-wide median income.

- *Or:* In the case of a tract located within a metropolitan area, the median family income for the area does not exceed 80% of the greater of the statewide family income or the metropolitan area median family income.

In the last chapter I promised I would tell you the number of residents of QOZs. Well, I won't keep you in suspense any longer.

Given the aforementioned criteria, one in six Americans reside in a dis-tressed urban, rural, or suburban community. This totals approximately *35 million people—*or *9.5% of our population—*who live in areas that can potentially be assisted by Subchapter Z of the tax bill. That is a gigantic population of people who are struggling to make ends meet, which truly makes this a unique and extraordinary endeavor.

C: Government Rules on How QOZs Are Nominated and Who Approves Them

We have identified *how* a QOZ is defined and *what* numbers enable a com-munity to qualify for the program. Now what's left is the *who* part of the equation—the people who nominate QOZs and then make the determina-tion *yes* or *no* for final approval.

Welcome to the letter *C* of our ABCs. If there weren't arbiters and processes in place, the QOZ approval process could potentially turn into a free-for-all and certain areas might end up on the receiving end of bias favoring (or disfavoring) one community over another. If such corruption were to occur, communities that aren't in need of such support would benefit, while those in dire situations would continue to suffer.

Fortunately, this isn't the case. The authors of the TCJA took great pains to ensure an even playing field and fairness for all types of urban and rural communities. Diving back into the document we discover the following language:

(A) not later than the end of the determination period, the chief executive officer of the State in which the tract is located—(i) nominates the tract for designation as a qualified opportunity zone, and (ii) notifies the Secretary in writing of such nomination, and

(B) the Secretary certifies such nomination and designates such tract as a qualified opportunity zone before the end of the consideration period.

This section lays out the approval process pretty well. The chief executive officer of a distressed area (i.e., the governor) selects and nominates certain population census tracts as low-income areas. The request then gets passed along to the U.S. Secretary of the Treasury, who must approve the application in order for it to be counted as a QOZ.

A Few Important Considerations

There are several additional things you must know. Eligible QOZs were based on 2011-2015 American Community Survey data from the Census Bureau, which identified over 41,000 population census tracts that were under consideration for designation as a QOZ. Next the TCJA applied a maximum number of designations of population census tracts a state may have that can be named QOZs. It cannot exceed 25% of the number of low-income communities in the state. There is an exception, however; if the number of low-income communities in a state is less than one hundred, then a total of twenty-five of such tracts may be designated as QOZs.

Additionally, the TCJA states that:

...a population census tract that is not a low-income community may be designated as a qualified opportunity zone under this section if (A) the

tract is contiguous with the low-income community that is designated as a qualified opportunity zone, and (B) the median family income of the tract does not exceed 125 percent of the median family income of the low-income community with which the tract is contiguous.

Attention QOZs—Please Step Forward!

Once all of the criteria were established, the government's next step was to begin the process of labeling the communities that qualified. On June 14, 2018, the Treasury and IRS announced the final round of designations for QOZs. The formal list, which is regularly updated, recognizes QOZs in all fifty states, the District of Columbia, American Samoa, Guam, the Northern Mariana Islands, Puerto Rico, and the Virgin Islands. A list and a map of the final QOZs may be accessed on the Treasury's Community Development Financial Institutions Fund website at: **https://www.cims.cdfifund.gov/preparation/?config=config_nmtc.xm.**

At this time, politicians and communities remain far too silent about QOZs and their benefits. Public awareness has been limited, with one notable exception. In February 2019, Vice President Mike Pence, second lady Karen Pence, and Senator Tim Scott attended an event in Columbia, SC celebrating the successful reopening of the local movie theater, which resulted from investments in this QOZ.

Pence declared to the audience: "No citizen will be forgotten. No community will be ignored…. No American will be left on the sidelines. We must unlock the potential of all our people, not just some of our people. And that's what Opportunity Zones are doing right here in Columbia."

How Many QOZs Are There as of Now?

You may be wondering: What does all of this add up to?

As of this writing, there are nearly *8,800 QOZs spanning all of the aforementioned areas,* which means that without a doubt there is an approved distressed community somewhere in your vicinity that can benefit from your investments.

The good news is that you don't need to reside in the QOZ to make a difference in one, although there are some established rules to follow regarding the specific businesses and types of properties involved—which will all be explained in the following chapter.

What Is QOZ Property (QOZP)?

There is a lot of intimidating jargon that surrounds QOZs, which we will explore in complete detail in Chapter Five. For now, before we draw the curtain on defining QOZs, you need to become familiar with some of this additional language—especially one central term: *QOZ Property (QOZP)*. Let's start with the verbiage used in the TCJA:

> *The term 'qualified opportunity zone property' means property which is—*
> *"(i) qualified opportunity zone stock,*
> *(ii) qualified opportunity zone partnership*
> *interest, or*
> *(iii) qualified opportunity zone business property..."*

Typical government double-speak: Qualified Opportunity Zone Property (QOZP) is defined with *three more technical phrases*! On the surface, the third one (iii) seems to be a real head-scratcher. Qualified Opportunity Zone Property consists of Qualified Opportunity Zone *Business* Property—how does that even begin to make sense?

Before our heads explode, let's unpack some of this language.

Qualified Opportunity Zone Stock (QOZS)

Qualified Opportunity Zone Stock (QOZS) refers to any stock in a domestic corporation, as long as it was acquired by a Qualified Opportunity Fund (QOF) after December 31, 2017 at its original issue—directly or through an underwriter—from the corporation solely in exchange for cash. The corporation must specifically be an existing or new QOZ Business (QOZB), a term that is defined in the next chapter.

Qualified Opportunity Zone Partnership Interest (QOZPI)

A Qualified Opportunity Zone Partnership Interest (QOZPI) refers to any equity interest in a partnership if such interest was acquired by a QOF after December 31, 2017 solely in exchange for cash. At the time such interest was acquired, the QOZPI had to be a QOZ Business (QOZB) used specifically for purposes directly associated with the approved area.

As you may have noticed, both QOZS and QOZPI must be issued from a QOZ Business (QOZB). So, what's a QOZ Business? Well, we'll discuss that more in the next chapter, but its primary qualifications are that:

- 70% of its tangible property is QOZ Business Property (defined below); and

- 50% of its gross income is derived from a QOZ, or 50% of its employees' or independent contractors' hours or pay are for work performed within a QOZ.

Qualified Opportunity Zone Business Property (QOZBP)

This is where things start to sound dicey. The term Qualified Opportunity Zone Business Property (QOZBP) refers to any tangible property—such as real estate and equipment—that has been purchased after December 31, 2017 and is substantially used all of the time in a QOZ and is part of a trade or business. This real estate, equipment, etc. must be used exclusively for QOZ purposes and be substantially improved after the purchase.

In summary, QOZBP must meet the following four criteria:

1. It must be used in the trade or business of a QOF.
2. It must be acquired by purchase after December 31, 2017.
3. It must either be originally used by the QOF in the QOZ or substantially improved by the QOF.
4. During substantially all of the time it is held by the QOF or the QOZB.

Now You Know Your ABCs of QOZs—and a Whole Lot More

Congratulations! You've officially graduated and can advance to Chapter Five: "Fun with Qualified Opportunity Funds (QOFs)." You will not only learn what QOFs are and how they function as the vehicle for investing in QOZs, you will discover how to position them to save a significant amount on capital gains tax, enabling you to begin mining all of the benefits of Subchapter Z of the TCJA.

FUN WITH QUALIFIED OPPORTUNITY FUNDS (QOFs)

We spent a lot of time in the last chapter explaining QOZs: what they are, how they were approved, and the total number of them that have been identified. We even defined the mumbo jumbo terminology related to them—so much, in fact, that by now you should have an honorary Ph.D. in understanding QOZs.

In this chapter, I'll further your education by guiding you through: what QOFs are; fund structure; and many of the tricky rules pertaining to QOFs. I'll also open your mind to all kinds of possibilities when it comes to QOFs, since there are some lesser known but lucrative opportunities available, in addition to the obvious ones (i.e., real estate). Of course, we'll have some fun with QOFs along the way.

Tighten your seatbelt: We've crammed a lot of important information into this chapter, and it's going to be a fast, bumpy ride with a lot of technical stuff I will do my best to simplify.

What Is a QOF?

You've probably figured out by now that a Qualified Opportunity Fund (QOF) is an investment vehicle created as part of the TCJA enacted in December 2017 to incentivize investment in QOZs—approved distressed areas. The purpose of this portion of the TCJA is to spur economic development, growth, and job creation in these communities utilizing QOFs as the tool. The program involves a mechanism that enables investors with capital gains tax liabilities to receive favorable tax treatment for investing in QOZs. There are many different kinds of QOFs available, such as: those that invest in commercial real estate; residential properties; retail, industrials, service and other types of businesses; and even start-up companies. For now, hold onto your britches a bit longer as we will cover all of this later in this chapter.

In a nutshell: Invest in QOZs via QOFs in your preferred business sector, and you can potentially save a fortune in capital gains tax over time. How about *that* for an incentive!

The exact definition of QOF in Subchapter Z is as follows:

The term "qualified opportunity fund" means any investment vehicle which is organized as a corporation or a partnership for the purpose of investing in qualified opportunity zone property (other than another qualified opportunity fund) that holds at least 90 percent of its assets in qualified opportunity zone property, determined by the average of the percentage of qualified opportunity zone property held in the fund as measured—

(A) on the last day of the first 6-month period of the taxable year of the fund, and

(B) on the last day of the taxable year of the fund...

Fortunately, we defined QOZ Property (QOZP) in the last chapter—so we're already halfway there. As a reminder, QOZP consists of QOZ Stock, QOZ Partnership Interest, and/or QOZ Business Property (QOZBP). The gist of the above paragraph is that at least 90% of the QOF's assets must be in the form of QOZ Property (QOZP), as determined by averages taken on the last day of the first six-month period of the taxable year of the fund and on the last day of the taxable year of the fund.

Now, why couldn't the authors of the clause have simply just written it that way? Well, bless their hearts—at least they tried.

How Can a QOF Benefit You and Me?

Some of you may believe the above heading is the most important part of this chapter—perhaps even of this entire book!—and are asking the obvious question: "So, Doc White, what's in it for me?"

It's perfectly okay to ask that question. We already made the case earlier in the book that there isn't any kind of ethical dilemma here. In my view, it doesn't matter if you're investing in QOFs out of the goodness of your heart, or if you are doing so to build wealth and helping others is just a side benefit. But don't worry. No one is suggesting you have to give everything away and then hope for the best. In other words, it's time for me to *show you the money*.

We've been building up to this promise right from the very first page of this book. First and foremost, the major benefit to investors and corporations investing in QOFs is all about these five words: *tax savings on capital gains*. The capital gains eligible for such tax savings includes those derived from the sale of *any asset*, including stock, real estate, equipment, etc.

There are four major benefits of investing capital gains into QOFs. Let's slice the apple in quarters, so we may take a look at each one individually.

A Capital Idea—Deferment

Here's how it works. Short- and long-term capital gains can be invested in QOFs to defer federal recognition of your capital gains up through December 31, 2026. You can then postpone paying the federal tax obligation until the tax return due date in 2027.

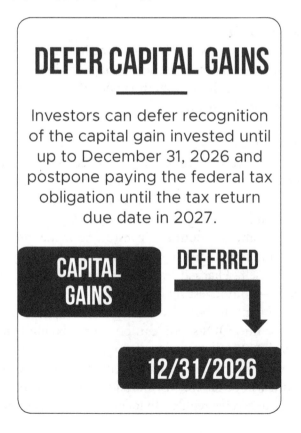

DEFER CAPITAL GAINS

Investors can defer recognition of the capital gain invested until up to December 31, 2026 and postpone paying the federal tax obligation until the tax return due date in 2027.

CAPITAL GAINS **DEFERRED**

12/31/2026

Reducing Your Taxable Gains

No, it's not a paradox, though it sounds like it: You can most certainly *reduce* your taxable capital *gains*. I told you we'd have fun with QOFs!

The federal taxable portion of the deferred capital gains may be reduced by up to 15%. It is very important to note that, if you want this *full 15% reduction* in the federal taxable portion of the deferred capital gains, you must invest in the QOF by December 31, 2019. The reason is that, in order to take the full 15% reduction, you must hold your investment for at least seven years prior to the tax-deferral end date of December 31, 2026. This breaks down to 10% if the investment is held for five years and an additional 5% if retained for seven years.

If you happen to be reading this after the December 31, 2019 date, do not be discouraged! You can still save a great deal on capital gains tax. Once the deadline has passed, you can still receive a 10% reduction as long as the investment is held for at least five years leading up to the December 31, 2026 end date.

No Pain, Lots of Gain

The benefits can get even better. If you, as the investor, hold your interest in the QOF for ten years and then sell it, any additional gain in excess of the deferred gain recognized in 2026 is *not subject to any federal income tax*. Patience is indeed a virtue!

And There's More . . .

Of course, as an investor, while you are deferring and reducing your capital gains tax obligations, you can still receive dividends or other income from investing in a QOF. The win-win-win-win is for the QOZ neighborhoods to improve, grow, and prosper; QOZ businesses to start (or restart), blossom, and flourish; investors to make money on capital gains deferrals and reductions; and for investors to actually make money from the QOF itself. That's at least *four wins*—a grand slam home run in any ballpark—from investing in a QOF.

What does this mean boiled down to one simple thing? By investing capital gains into QOFs, you can postpone paying federal taxes on such gains until 2027; the amount of gains subject to tax will go down 10-15%; any appreciation on your QOF interest over the deferred capital gain amount will be tax free if you hold it for ten years; and you have an opportunity to receive regular dividend income along the way. At the

REDUCE TAXABLE GAINS

The capital gain subject to federal tax can be reduced by up to 15%* (10% if the investment is held for 5 years and an additional 5% if held for 7 years). *You MUST invest capital gains no later than December 31, 2019 to take the FULL 15% Capital Gain for Reduction.

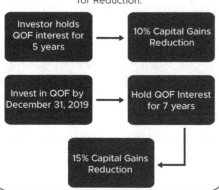

ELIMINATE ADDITIONAL CAPITAL GAIN TAXES

If the investor holds the QOF investment for 10 years, any additional gain (in excess of the deferred gain recognized in 2026) on the sale of such QOF investment is not subject to federal income tax if sold prior to 2048.

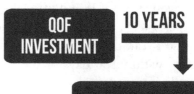

Additional Gains 100% Tax-free

RECEIVE INCOME DISTRIBUTIONS

Investors might also receive income distributions from the QOF's earnings.

QOF INVESTMENT

↓

QOF EARNINGS

↓

INCOME

QOF INVESTMENTS AFTER 2021

✓ If a QOF investment is made after 12/31/2021, no capital gain reductions will be available.

✓ HOWEVER, if the investor holds the QOF interest for at least 10 years, any appreciation thereof (in excess of the deferred gain recognized in 2026) is 100% federal tax-free if sold prior to 2048.

same time, you will feel good that you are part of something remarkable—the rebirth of an entire distressed community that was crumbling and otherwise looking at a dismal future, if not for your contributions.

Around the QOFs in 180 Days

The next principle to understand is that you must invest in a QOF within *180 days* of recognizing the eligible capital gain. For example, each time an entity sells stock for a capital gain, it has 180 days from the sale thereof to invest in a QOF. Additionally, if a company sells real or depreciable property (e.g., real estate, equipment, or other depreciable assets) during its fiscal year, that company may invest the net "IRC Section 1231 capital gains" within 180 days of the end of such year. If you choose to invest the eligible capital gain in a QOF, you simply need to make the deferral election by filing a form with your U.S. federal income tax return. The alternative, of course, is to pay federal capital gains taxes in full and earlier than necessary.

QUALIFIED OPPORTUNITY FUNDS

Investors must invest in a QOF within 180 days of recognizing the eligible capital gain. The alternative option is to pay federal taxes on the capital gain.

INVEST IN

QOF

Within 180 days of recognizing capital gain

OR

Pay federal taxes on capital gain

If the investor chooses to invest the eligible capital gain in a QOF, the individual MUST make the deferral election by filing a form with his or her US federal income tax return for the year in which the deferred gain would have been recognized.

Special Rules

SEC. 1400Z–2 of Subchapter Z outlines a series of "Special Rules for Capital Gains Invested in Opportunity Zones." As mentioned earlier in this chapter, a QOF must invest 90% of its assets in QOZP. (This is known as the "90% *asset test*," for those interested in knowing all of the verbiage.) This requirement may be satisfied by acquiring QOZ Business Property (QOZBP) directly or indirectly through the acquisition of the stock or partnership interest of a QOZ Business (QOZB) that holds the QOZBP. In the latter scenario, a QOZ Business needs only to hold at least seventy percent (70%) of its tangible assets as QOZBP. (Guess what? Surprise—this is known as the "70% *asset test*.")

Getting Down and Dirty with QOZBPs

So, now we know that QOZ Business Property (QOZBP) is the underlying asset that must be held either directly by a QOF (90% *asset test*) or by a QOZ Business invested in by a QOF (70% *asset test*). Now, let's revisit QOZBPs introduced in Chapter Four.

Generally speaking, QOZ Business Property is tangible property (real or personal property) *used in a trade or business* in the QOZ where either:

- The *"original use"* of the property commences with the QOF or QOZ Business;

or

- The QOF or QOZ Business *"substantially improves"* the property, which means doubling the basis in the property.

There are exceptions and nuances to these rules. Below are some examples of potential QOZBPs, and how the regulations are applied in different scenarios.

Note: In order to make the language less cumbersome, repetitive-sounding, and confusing, I've intentionally left off "or QOZ Business (QOZB)" when referring to a QOF in every sentence. Be aware that all conditions below apply to both QOF and QOZB.

1. Building—*original use* test

   • A new building built by the QOF in a QOZ; *or*

   • A building in a QOZ that has been vacant for at least five years; *or*

   • A building that is partially completed, as long as the QOF is the first to place it into service in the QOZ for purposes of amortization or depreciation.

   Example: A QOF purchases a partially completed building—such as an office building, hotel, factory, etc.—completes the construction, and puts it into service in the QOZ for the first time. As described in the third bullet above, it has never before been amortized or depreciated by any taxpayer in a QOZ and would therefore pass the test.

2. Building—*Substantially Improved Test*
   A QOF may purchase an existing building and satisfy the *substantially improved test* by adhering to the following stipulations:

   • The QOF must double the basis in the property. For example, if the building costs $400,000, then at least another $400,000 must be invested toward improving the building; *and*

   • The QOF must complete the improvements within a thirty-month period.

   You should note that the land portion of the real estate purchase is excluded from both the *original use* and *substantial improvement* tests. The value of the land is not used in the "double the basis" requirement cited in the first bullet, above.

   Example: A QOF purchases real estate located in a QOZ for $1 million with $600,000 of such purchase price allocable to land and $400,000 allocable to an existing building. In this instance, the land is not part of the *original use* requirement.

   Assuming the building does not qualify under the original use requirement—as mentioned, a new building constructed by the QOF, one that has been vacant for over five years, or a partially completed new building—it must be *substantially improved* in order to qualify as QOZBP. Therefore, for this real estate—both the land and building—to qualify, the QOF must spend at least $400,000 on improvements to the building to double the $400,000 basis in the building. In this example, 100% of the assets would be QOZBP because the land is excluded from both the *original use* and *substantial improvement* requirements.

3. Types of Buildings—*trade or business test*
In order for a building to count as QOZ Business Property (QOZBP), it must be used by the QOF exclusively in an active "trade or business" as defined by IRC Section 162 (which basically means it generates deductible business expenses).

In other words, the QOF must own and operate the building for business purposes. Here are just a few examples of buildings that may be owned and operated by the QOF:

• Airplane hangars.

• Apartment complexes with full service gross leases.

• Condo/town home complexes with full service gross leases.

• Dealerships.

• Education: schools and libraries.

• Factories.

• Fast food restaurants.

• Food processing facilities.

• Hotels and motels.

• Manufacturing facilities.

• Movie theaters.

• Office buildings with full gross leases.

• Packing sheds.

• Performing arts centers and concert halls.

• Shops and retail stores.

• Strip malls.

- Warehouses and cold storage facilities.

- And more!

For QOZBs (such as QOZ stock or QOZ partnership entities owned by QOFs, but not the QOFs themselves), there are some notable exclusions based on...*ahem*...a certain type of business referred to as a "sin business." The following are pretty self-explanatory: liquor stores, massage parlors (and anything of the like, you get the picture), tanning salons, and gambling establishments. Also branded with the label "sin businesses" are golf courses and country clubs. Don't ask me why—I didn't make the rules! Fortunately, this exclusion does not apply to the QOFs, which can directly own a sin business.

Okay, let's see how good you are at interpreting IRS-speak with a quick quiz.

Which of the following examples below would be considered a QOZBP building that may be deducted? Choose more than one answer, if applicable:

A. Your dog Fido's doghouse located in the QOZ.
B. The writing space in which I wrote this book located in a QOZ.
C. Cousin Kato's guest room located in a house in the QOZ. (Let's assume Kato is an employee of your business in the QOZ and not a freeloader.)
D. A building you purchased and refurbished in the QOZ. The top floors are affordable apartments, while the storefront on the street level is a remodeled tobacco shop. All have full service gross leases.

Answer: Only *D* would qualify as a deduction. In case you thought it was a trick: Tobacco is not considered a "sin business." I was just having some fun with the other three options.

It is also possible for the QOF to purchase and/or lease commercial and residential buildings to third parties. In the case of a lease, the type must be a full service gross lease and not a triple net (NNN) lease (one in which the tenant is completely responsible for all costs, including the rent; taxes; building insurance; and maintenance fees).

4. Land

Any land purchased by a QOF in a QOZ must be an active trade or business. Buying and holding land for re-sale purposes will not qualify.

Land is not counted in the *original use* or *substantial improvement* tests if purchased along with a building that passes such tests. However, land can qualify as a QOZBP if purchased on its own according to the following current rules:

- Land acquired in a QOZ does not need to meet the *original use* test, whether improved or unimproved.

- Land acquired in a QOZ that is unimproved does not need to meet the *substantial improvement* test.

- However, land acquired in a QOZ that is already improved must meet the *substantial improvement* test just like a building. An example of this would be adding infrastructure to improved land within thirty months so that it doubles the basis of the land.

5. Tangible Personal Property

Tangible personal property used in a QOZ constitutes QOZBP if it passes either the *original use* test or the *substantial improvement* test and is used in a trade or business.

In order for new tangible personal property to pass the *original use* test, it must be put into service and amortized or depreciated for the first time by a QOF in the QOZ. For example, a twelve-pallet forklift purchased by a QOF and operated in a QOZ for the first time would qualify. The QOF may also enter a full-service lease of such forklift with a company located in a QOZ, as long as the leasing of the machinery is part of the QOF's active trade or business.

For *substantial improvement* of personal property (e.g., equipment), the QOF must double the basis in the property (in other words, invest the purchase price or more to improve the personal property). A fictionalized example of this would be for a QOF to purchase Candy's Candy used delivery truck for $1,500 and convert it into Willy Vanilli's ice cream truck by investing $1,500 or more in renovations. The ice cream truck would serve one hundred flavors of premium ice cream—including a dozen varieties of vanilla—to delighted kids on the steamy streets of a QOZ situated in Tempe, Arizona.

For used tangible personal property, in order to pass the *original use* test, it must not have been previously used in the QOZ in a manner that would have allowed it to be amortized or depreciated by a taxpayer. A fictionalized example of this would be for a QOF to purchase the famous "Big Cheese" food truck (serving grilled cheese sandwiches, of course), which had been a longtime staple in Madison, Wisconsin. The used Big Cheese truck (the vehicle having been "used," not the cheese, of course) is being transplanted to a QOZ area located in West Oakland, CA, so it passes the test.

6. Property Leased by a QOF
   A lease of property by a QOF that is inside a QOZ qualifies as QOZBP under the following circumstances:

   • Tangible property leased from an *unrelated* party does not need to satisfy either the *original use* test or the *substantial improvement* test. An example of this would be a QOF leasing an office inside a QOZ from an unrelated party for five years at $5,000 per month.

     • A lease from a *related* party has the following restrictions and requirements:

     • No pre-payments of rent exceeding 12 months; and

     • The property must satisfy the *original use* test;

     or

     • During the thirty-month period after the lease start date, the QOF must acquire other tangible QOZBP with a value equal to that of the leased property. Note that this other QOZBP doesn't have to be related to the leased premises, and the "value" of the lease can either be the present value of all lease payments or the value per the financial statement (see below).

   • A lease with an option to purchase from either a related or unrelated party is allowed, as long as the Fair Market Value (FMV) purchase price is determined at the time of the purchase.

- The QOF may value leased QOZBP by using either: the financial statement valuation method; or the present value of all lease payments. Under the financial statement valuation method, the value of the leased property is as reported on the applicable financial statement if prepared in accordance with generally accepted accounting principles (GAAP). Under the present value method, the value of a leased tangible property is equal to the sum of the present values of each payment under the lease calculated at the time the QOF enters into the lease (discounted at the applicable Federal rate under IRC Section 1274(d)(1)).

All of these stipulations are necessary to know, but I apologize if they inadvertently gave you a brain cramp. I'm sure you are grateful that we are next moving on to the action items of this chapter: *how* a QOF can invest in a QOZ Business (QOZB), which is in and of itself a QOZP, as long as it meets certain requirements as discussed below.

How Can a QOF Invest in a QOZB?

A QOF can invest in a QOZB in a couple of different ways. First, it may acquire stock or partnership interest from an existing corporation or partnership that is already a QOZB. The QOF must acquire such stock or partnership interest directly from a QOZB (or an underwriter) as part of an original issuance of such stock or partnership interest, rather than from a current shareholder or partner.

Alternatively, the QOF can form a new corporation or partnership (startup) that is established to become a QOZB.

What Are the QOZB Requirements?

In order for a corporation or partnership to qualify as a QOZB, several requirements must be met. I'll try to make this rundown a simple sprint rather than a marathon to get through.

First, 70% of its tangible property—owned or leased—must be QOZ

Business Property (QOZBP). Second, at least 50% of its total gross income—including bank interest on working capital—must be derived from the active conduct of its business in a QOZ (we'll call that the "50% test"). The 50% test can be met in *any one* of the following ways:

- If at least 50% of the hours spent by employees and independent contractors are within the QOZ, the test is satisfied.

Example:

- If a QOZ Business' employees are all located in a QOZ, it doesn't matter where the customers are located, the business will meet the test.

- If at least 50% of the amount paid by a QOZ Business to employees and independent contractors are for services performed within a QOZ, the test is satisfied.

Example:

- A QOZ Business can have employees outside the QOZ, provided at least half of the total compensation is paid to employees performing services within the QOZ.

- If the tangible property located in a QOZ and the management or operational functions performed in the QOZ are each necessary for the generation of at least 50% of the gross income of the business, the test is satisfied.

It is important to know that no more than 5% of the entity's average adjusted basis in its property may be attributable to certain financial assets, such as debt, stock, partnership interests, and various financial instruments—but excluding reasonable working capital. While we are on this subject, take special note of reasonable working capital. Cash of QOZB does not count towards this 5% limit if the entity has a written schedule of how cash will be deployed to acquire eligible assets in the QOZ within thirty-one months. The cash must be deployed in a *substantially consistent* manner with that schedule.

Direct QOF Ownership Vs. Owning Equity in a QOZB

The following table is a comparison between a QOF holding QOZBP directly versus a QOF owning stock or partnership interest in a QOZB: Here is an example of how this plays out:

- The QOF receives a $10 million investment.

- The QOF allocates 10% of this amount ($1 million) towards working capital, and invests the required 90% minimum ($9 million) either:

  - Directly into QOZBP; *and/or*

  - Into stock or partnership interests of a QOZB that is a newly formed QOF subsidiary and/or an existing QOZB directly issuing equity.

- Assuming the QOF invests the $9M into one or more QOZBs as the only funds invested therein, then the QOZBs can use the $9M from the QOF as follows:

  - All $9M can remain in the bank so long as the QOZB has a plan to acquire eligible assets in a QOZ within thirty-one months and deploy the cash *substantially consistent* with that plan.

  - When it does deploy the capital, the QOZ Business—unlike a QOF—is only required to have 70% of its tangible property as QOZBP.

  - The QOZB can also have unlimited intangible property, as long as 40% of it is used in the conduct of business in the QOZB.

What Areas Are Ripe for QOF Investments?

Outside all of the aforementioned stipulations, the sky is the limit for QOF investing! The possibilities are endless—all you need to do is tap into your imagination. Most funds currently focus on real estate, but there

WHAT ARE THE DIFFERENCES BETWEEN A QOF DIRECTLY OWNING QOZ BUSINESS PROPERTY VS. OWNING EQUITY IN QOZ BUSINESS THAT OWNS QOZ BUSINESS PROPERTY?

The following table is a comparison between a QOF holding QOZ Business Property ("QOZBP") directly versus a QOF owning stock or partnership interests in a QOZ Business.

Note: This comparison is from a QOF (not an investor) standpoint. It is the benefit of a QOF owning QOZBP directly versus owning the same through a QOZ Business.

	QOF Directly Owns QOZBP	QOF Business
Working Capital:	10% Max (90% Minimum in QOZBP)	Greater than 10% if written schedule of up to 31 months & investment consistent therewith
Intangible Property:	Must be part of 10% above	Unlimited, so long as used in active conduct of QOZ business
Timing Issues:	Must acquire QOZBP in time to meet 90% Asset Tests	Investing in QOZ Business meets test if the cash is designated for construction, acquisition or substantial improvement of QOZ Property with 31 mo. schedule to do so
Amount of QOZBP:	90% Minimum	Tangible Property must meet 70% Minimum, allowing for QOZ Business to hold up to 30% in Non-QOZBP
Income Percentage:	No restrictions	At least 50% from active QOZ business (working capital bank interest counts towards this), unless meets other 50% tests.
Type of Property:	90% Tangible - QOZBP	Tangible or Intangible OK
Type of Activity:	No restriction	"Sin" Business limits as previously defined

are numerous other major opportunities that tend to get overlooked. A lot has to do with what is available, promising, and requires nurturing in the QOZ that falls into your comfort zone, investment strategy, and personal areas of interest.

I cannot emphasize enough the versatility and wide-ranging areas QOFs can cover. You can consider QOFs that focus on manufacturing, warehousing, equipment dealerships, management consulting, accounting and financial services, a commercial building, affordable residential housing, a coffee bar, a movie theater, a bowling alley, a skating rink, a sneaker store, a jewelry store, a pet store, a clothing boutique, a bike store/repair shop, a hardware store, a candy store, a food truck, and on and on. While we're on the subject of "ripe," why not a fruit stand?

There are many creative ways to build a QOF structure. For example, it is possible to create QOF business subsidiaries to provide management consulting services to businesses within a QOZ. Or, it could focus on investing in startup companies within a QOZ. Alternatively, a QOF may want to specialize in acquisitions and turnarounds of existing companies within one or more QOZs.

The QOF could even partner with non-profits to provide community improvements within a QOZ, such as parks and green spaces. Don't forget: The QOF receives an additional tax deduction for investing in a non-profit. As I wrote no less than twice before in this chapter by intent, the possibilities are endless....

You are ready to rock and roll! I've now shared with you what QOFs are and the basic rules you need to know in order to invest in them, such as the 180-day requirement to invest capital gains. You are also familiar with all of the many benefits that can be mined from investing the capital gains in QOFs that invest in QOZPs: deferral and reduction of tax obligations; tax-free appreciation over the original investment; and opportunity to generate income from QOF earnings. You understand that QOFs can be flexible and that you are not limited to investing in QOFs that focus on just real estate. You can direct the funds toward whatever your investment strategy dictates, your heart desires, and your comfort zone allows, as long as the investments comply with the rules.

I only have one thing left to accomplish in this chapter: Offer my hearty congratulations to you for having crossed the finish line. Now that you are well-versed in the main principles of QOFs, you are all set to advance to Part Three and start making a difference!

PART THREE

MAKING A DIFFERENCE

CHAPTER SIX

REVITALIZING COMMUNITIES

In Part Two we covered the ins and outs of how you can utilize QOFs as a vehicle to invest in QOZs in order to make significant dollars and profit through tax benefits, capital gains savings, and return on investment. I think we've well established that I do not believe capitalism is a bad thing and I, for one, am not in any way against you or anyone making money (as long as it's earned ethically and legally, of course).

Now we have arrived at Part Three. I believe this chapter and the next are so important that they could be expanded to form a standalone book. (Someday I may just do that!)

All of this means that it is time for you to truly connect your brain and heart and make a genuine positive difference in these communities. Each day the message becomes increasingly critical. The distressed urban and rural communities in QOZs have unique needs, and they urgently need help (not handouts, mind you). These areas are not going to improve by themselves. The leaders of America have generally been absent in this regard. Neither they—nor we—can sit on the sidelines while our communities sink.

If America can't help them, what kind of example are we setting for the rest of the world that has a lower standard of living?

Your Values Really Do Matter

Cory Booker once said, "If you look at great human civilizations, from the Roman Empire to the Soviet Union, you will see that most do not fail simply due to external threats but because of internal weakness, corruption, or a failure to manifest the values and ideals they espouse."

A person's definition of "values" can be debated. I have grounded my life and work in my values, which I define as follows:

- Tell the truth.

- Do what you say.

- Lead by example.

- Conduct your business with integrity.

- Be accountable.

Your definition may be a restatement or a variation of the above. However you phrase your personal definition of the word *values*, having them sets a high bar that is not easy to maintain day in and day out. But make no mistake: All of us have a responsibility to demonstrate our core values not just in our private lives, but also in business and for our communities.

As you will soon discover later on in this chapter, there are numerous ways for you to apply your virtuous efforts toward communities. QOFs can be devoted to philanthropic activities in QOZs just as easily as for-profit businesses. The message is clear: You can target your favorite charities within a QOZ, partnering and supporting them in multiple improvement efforts.

It all comes down to this: *a call to action.* Time is slipping through our fingers, which means we must act now. Let's get together on this major issue to create a new and better future for these urban and rural communities of our great nation!

A Case Study: The Faded American Dream

Before I probe the specifics of how QOFs can help revitalize QOZ communities, bear with me as I introduce a community case study that begs attention. The QOZ about to be discussed in the following sections is real, although you may wonder why I selected this one particular area as an example. To be sure, I could have chosen any one of a number of the 8,800 some-odd examples and made the same point.

Mark my words: This QOZ is *special.* Not because I lived there, know anyone there, or have even invested or conducted business there. As it happens, as of this writing, the answer would be "no" to each of these three circumstances.

This particular QOZ was selected because at one time it was symbolic of the American Dream. It is located pretty much right in the heart of our country. Many years ago, it was a prosperous and thriving community with a bright future. It produced and manufactured invaluable commodities essential for our country's economic growth and development as a world power.

Now, unfortunately, it is a hotbed of socio-economic issues and the community is in dire need of revitalization. Being identified with QOZ areas affords it an extraordinary opportunity to turn things around and bring back a glimmer of the American Dream.

When Youngstown, OH Was Young

Youngstown: a town in Northeastern Ohio that was first founded in 1797 by a pioneer from New York named, fittingly enough, John Young. It was incorporated five years later and has since become a county seat of Mahoning County.

Clearly, Young saw the potential in the area, purchasing 15,560 acres of land for just over $16K. Adjusted for inflation to today, that amount would be worth upward of $309 million. Talk about a tidy sum!

As soon as iron ore and coal deposits were discovered near the area, Youngstown began to blossom. The iron industry thrived, the railroads chugged back and forth through it, steel mills were constructed, and the population soared. Employment opportunities drew immigrants hailing from a wide variety of nations, including Poland, Italy, and Hungary. Between 1890 and 1930, Youngstown exploded from 33,000 residents to 170,000.

As a result of the boom, two favorable monikers were applied to the town during the years that followed. It came to be known as part of "the Rust Belt"—an obvious reference to its role as one of the nation's leading providers of steel and other metals. Along with similar towns, it was referred to as "the Industrial Heartland of North America." Workers at Republic Steel (founded as the Republic Iron and Steel Company in Youngstown), the U.S. Steel Ohio Works, and Youngstown Sheet and Tube toiled around the clock to meet the country's substantial product and manufacturing demands during the Industrial Revolution.

Youngstown suffered along with the rest of the country during the Great Depression, but then rebounded amidst World War II when steel was singled out as a valuable commodity for creating weapons and machinery to support the military effort. The city returned to serving a vital role as one of the nation's leading providers of steel and other important metals.

Once again, Youngstown was prosperous with a growing population. For many people, the town symbolized the American Dream with opportunities available for anyone willing to put in the hard work.

An Offer That Should Have Been Refused

As you've no doubt been expecting, the picture stopped being so rosy for Youngstown. The first hammer to fall was the national steel strike of 1959. The situation damaged the area's economy and workforce so badly the press dubbed Youngstown "Steel's Sick City." (Unlike the other two aforementioned nicknames, this one was evidently *not* intended to be favorable.) As if that wasn't enough, the community that had prided itself on diversity from its immigration-driven heritage and workforce became heavily segregated between black and white people with the economic burdens disproportionately hurting the former (as always seems to be the case).

By the late 1970s-early 80s, Youngstown faced global competition and demand for its steel dwindled. The visible pollution from the factories gradually began to fade away, replaced by a malaise felt by the entire community caused by downward trends and joblessness. To make matters worse, the Mafia overtook many aspects of local government; corruption reigned supreme right up through the end of the millennium.

Although the FBI eventually straightened out the Mafia issue, other types of criminal activity continued to run rampant, which pretty much brings us up to date...

The Numbers Tell the Story

Remember just a few pages ago I wrote that the population of Youngstown in 1930 was 170,000? Well, take a wild guess as to what that number is today.

Based on the subsequent history of area declines, you probably figured the population has withstood a major hit. Did you guess 150,000? 125,000? 100,000?

Nope, nope, and nope. If you'd guessed *half* of the 1930 number it would still be way over. The correct number is a mere *64,609* people as of this writing—and continuing to plummet. Although the national population has increased nearly 4% over the past five years, Youngstown has actually *slipped 3.3%* in that same time frame.

The earnings picture is equally as bleak. The average household income is around $24K, less than half of the national average. The poverty rate is nearly 36%. (For those who don't like doing math, here's the translation: That is more than one out of every three people.) As insult to injury, although many of the old factories and warehouses are gone, the air quality is still below the national average for almost every day of the calendar year—a leftover "gift" from the industrial past.

Brother, Can You Spare a Dime—or a Job?

It all comes back to jobs: If there are no factories, there are limited places that can employ people in this area. As we've described in previous chapters, people head out in droves when jobs are scarce. This all comes full circle: When populations decline in an area, new businesses don't look to set up shop there.

Back in Chapter Two we established that the national unemployment rate is 3.6% at this time. Here are some sobering facts about Youngstown:

- Unemployment is more than double the national average at 7.7%.

- The city has the highest unemployment rate among areas with a population of 50,000 or more.

- Approximately 1,600 people are unemployed in the city limits alone.

Crime, Drugs, and Backed Up Sewage—Oh My!

Equally as alarming is the area's crime rate. If you are a resident of Youngstown, you have a 1 in 145 chance of being a victim of a violent crime—more than double the state's average. On the crime scale, the city rates an "8," which would be good if the parameters only went to "10."

Unfortunately, that's *8 out of 100* with the latter representing the safe end. In a nutshell: The crime rate for the area is well above the national average, while the violent crime rate is *135% higher* than the national average. In nearly every category, Youngstown has a greater criminal rate than Ohio and the nation overall: murder, robbery, assault, burglary, and property crime, to name a few.

Drugs are a significant problem in Youngstown, although this is obviously not unique in America in our present day and age. The city reports approximately fifty drug-related deaths per year—which is high for a population of its size—mostly due to heroin overdose. Along with suffering caused by this and opioid addiction, the following substances are also heavily abused: alcohol, marijuana, crack (and powder) cocaine, sedatives, and methamphetamines.

Here's another shocking fact: *One out of every four people fail employment drug tests.* How is the community ever going to get back on its feet and employed if its workers are constantly falling *under* their feet?

Not to dump on Youngstown, but the city has also had its share of sewage and other infrastructure issues. Back in Fall 2018, Mahoning County experienced massive sewage backups. The frequent muck in basements became so intolerable on Water Street that residents began to refer to their own area as "Sewage Street."

The cause? You guessed it: old, aging pipes and not enough money and resources to take care of them.

What Is This QOZ Doing to Help Itself?

We've established that Youngstown, OH once represented the American Dream for many people and has since fallen upon terribly hard times. Even so, you are probably still wondering why I have allotted so much time and attention to tell its story—drugs, sewage, and all.

For one reason only: This QOZ—like so many others—is well worth the investment and revitalization effort. The community has significant pride in its history and the many accomplishments that have sprung from the region over the years. Our country would not be the same if not for Youngstown, OH. In fact, one might ponder whether we would have even survived World War II without the city's steely contributions.

Picture this: Wouldn't it be remarkable to live to see Youngstown, OH reclaim some of its former glory? Is it even possible for the area to rebound and once again attract a population of 100,000 residents?

Granted, it is doubtful that even Youngstown itself would choose to lead the charge for a re-establishment of the Rust Belt and its smoky factories. While the job opportunities would be welcomed, the negative impacts of them on the environment—i.e., air quality and clean water supply—are probably not things anyone is clamoring to restore.

The good news is that the area is starting to diversify and many other avenues of investment have been sprouting: aluminum, biomedical, health care, and food products, etc. On the community improvement front, several initiatives have already been set in motion:

- The Chamber Foundation: In 2016, the Economic Development team collaborated on $1 billion in local investments.

- Investor Promotional Program: Offers promotional services, social media messaging, and news releases touting goods or services. A portion of sales garnered during the promotional period is allocated to the Foundation.

- Drive It Home Campaign: Created to assist nearby Lordstown, OH with the loss of worker shifts at the General Motors plant.

The above are truly creative and inspiring programs. There is no doubt that Mahoning County is well aware of the socio-economic situation and QOZ status of Youngstown and is taking significant steps to move forward and help its own cause. On the communal website[1], the Youngstown/Warren Regional Chamber specifically encourages QOZ investment in the area through tax credits from the TCJA. The Chamber leadership offers to help investors do the following: identify deal flow; coordinate local funds; point out applicable incentives; connect with developers/companies/investable business opportunities; collaborate with local elected officials; and track down additional support from local investors, lenders, bankers, and service providers. The website even has a map of consensus tract websites in the area highlighting specific QOZ territories.

---

1 Located at: **http://www.regionalchamber.com/initiativesprograms/opportunity-zones**

Invest in Communities That Are Committed to Themselves

If you are looking to invest in a specific location that is meaningful to you and qualifies as a QOZ, there is a likely chance that leadership in the community is familiar with Subchapter Z and will welcome you with open arms and provide resources and support, much like the Youngstown/Warren Regional Chamber. As you evaluate the swath of potential QOZ areas where you may invest in QOFs, investigate how much effort the local leadership is putting forth to advance its own improvement.

A QOZ that acknowledges the tax benefits of TCJA and provides time, energy, and resources to attract businesses is an excellent place to begin your investment analysis. In a sense, investing in a QOZ is like any other investment in that the prospects *must have a good story to tell.*

Ask yourself this important question: Which community's story appeals to you? As you consider the right QOZ, you will want to target an area that has a history you can relate to; is taking active steps to improve itself; and is building up businesses that fit in with your portfolio and strategic plan. Most of all, you want to find a community that concentrates on the future while celebrating its past, as can be seen in the example of Youngstown, OH.

If a community demonstrates passion for its own welfare and future success, you can feel confident that it will be committed for the long haul. Most importantly, of course, their passion will be contagious and resonate with you as well.

How Can Your Investment Help a QOZ Fly High?

Investing in QOFs situated in QOZs can deliver a substantial number of lasting benefits to a community. The obvious point is that your money, time, and energy will go toward business creation, job expansion, and other resulting improvements in that area (all of which I will cover, I promise!). The chain of events from there is as follows:

- One Investor ➜ *Multiple Investors*

- Multiple Investors ➜ *Business Growth*

- Business Growth ➜ *Increased Jobs*

- Increased Jobs ➜ *Population Expansion*

- Population Expansion ➜ *More Businesses*

This sequence can be taken even further and have the effect of a *fly-wheel*. In engineering-speak, a flywheel is a mechanical object that is used to increase a machine's momentum. The more effort and energy applied to the flywheel, the faster it goes and the greater the output. Below is the rippling jolt a community receives when its populations and businesses are given a boost.

POPULATION EXPANSION + MORE BUSINESSES

=

1. ECONOMIC GROWTH

2. BUSINESS INNOVATION

3. COMMUNITY IMPROVEMENTS

4. INFRASTRUCTURE IMPROVEMENTS

5. CRACKDOWN ON DRUGS, GANGS, AND CRIME

6. IMPROVED HEALTH CARE

7. IMPROVED ENVIRONMENTAL AND FOOD SAFETY

8. IMPROVED EDUCATION

9. MORE EFFECTIVE GOVERNMMENT

10. PRIDE IN COMMUNITY

11. BETTER QUALITY OF LIFE

12. COMMITMENT TO THE FUTURE

=

EVEN *GREATER* POPULATION EXPANSION + EVEN *MORE* BUSINESSES

All of these benefits don't happen overnight—but that is okay. As stated right in the beginning of this chapter, the QOZ designations remain in force until 2028. That offers plenty of time for a neighborhood to experience a complete makeover.

Once those dozen benefits in the chain start to take shape and materialize, business people and residents alike will become firsthand witnesses as the town comes alive. Trust will be built among the main stakeholders—businesses, investors, citizens, and officials—and a whole new story about the QOZ will be ready to be told.

Attention all communities such as the Youngstown, Ohios of America: Are you ready to build your flywheel?

What Does It Really Mean to Revitalize Communities?

Revitalizing Communities: This sounds like a pretty daunting task. How do we begin to tackle such a thing? When it comes down to it, we are talking about the *social benefits* of investing in QOFs to help QOZs and the impact of such improvements for the people living and/or working in those distressed areas. This has a ripple effect, speaking directly to the mental, emotional, and physical health of millions of people. If the communities are doing well, so will its residents and workforce.

In the remainder of this chapter, we are going to delve into specific ways QOFs can partner with entities in QOZs to repair and revitalize some of the most challenging issues these communities face. We'll take a look at real-life examples of how QOF investments have already been effectively applied to a diverse range of community-related areas:

- Non-profits and Philanthropy.

- Education.

- Infrastructure.

- Gang Violence.

- Health Care.

I must stress that by no means does this suggest that there aren't countless other examples already set in motion that have yet to take shape and be shared with the world. (You'll have to wait for my next book for those!) What follows represents only a fraction of the potential for what is possible in QOZs. In fact, affordable residential and commercial housing is part and parcel of many of these efforts, as you will see. It is my hope that on reading these scenarios you will be inspired to *take specific creative action* to place your investments in QOFs in order to make a difference in these distressed rural and urban QOZ communities.

Friends, this is not a pipe dream. QOF investments have already worked miracles in several American communities and we are only at the early stages of experiencing their capabilities. The way I see it, the only issue is excessive deliberation leading to inaction.

Now I know what you are thinking: *Doc White—what about helping out the businesses in the QOZs? When are you going to get to them?*

Have no fear! We will show how QOFs can revitalize businesses in the very next chapter…

It's Not What You Say, It's What You DO

The above heading is a twist on a well-known quote by steel tycoon Andrew Carnegie from over a century ago: "As I grow older, I pay less attention to what men say. I just watch what they do."

From my perspective, investing in QOFs to partner with non-profits and philanthropic organizations is one of the finest ways to directly influence a community and make a difference—one that can be seen and felt. This is all about tangible results from your actions, not just talk about generosity in giving to charitable causes and getting grants, hospital wings, and buildings named after you (not that there is anything wrong with any of that).

Most rural and urban towns already have existing non-profits that are worth investigating and contacting. If they are in QOZs, chances are they have been struggling to stay afloat, pay bills, and offer the full extent of services outlined in their charters. Perhaps some have even been shuttered due to debt and lack of funding; that shouldn't hinder you from seeing how you can become involved and bring them back to life by investing in QOFs to assist them.

Let's commence by proposing a few likely non-profits that may be found in QOZs. For example, nearly every town has a community center that offers programs for families—from children to seniors—as well as social support for people with financial or physical challenges. Not every one has a religious affiliation, though; if they do, chances are they are welcoming to people inside and outside their faiths. What if your QOFs were directed to help refurbish air-conditioned, wheelchair accessible buses to transport senior citizens to and from the community center? Or offer a summer program for kids whose families cannot afford day care and/or day camp?

All of that seems to make a great deal of obvious sense, right? Now let's really dive in. At one time or another many towns in low-income areas have had girls and boys clubs to help the community's children stay physically, mentally, and emotionally healthy and active. I can only imagine how many of these organizations fell into ruin during the last recession and never fully recovered. What happened to all of those children who had nothing to do for an entire summer—did they fall prey to drugs, gangs, and violence?

Now picture this scenario: You invest in a QOF supporting a boys and girls club in a QOZ. The chains are removed from the doors of the rundown building. The building gets gutted, repaired, and restored from the inside out with fresh coats of paint. The floor of the gymnasium basketball court is replaced and fresh nets are added to the basketball hoops. The weeds are cleared off a field out back and new chalk lines are drawn to form a baseball diamond. Suddenly, the boys and girls of this community have a place to go all-year round, instead of becoming prey on crime-ridden streets.

By the same token, you can leverage your investment money in QOFs to directly partner with non-profits and assist communities. Habitat for Humanity, for example, bought a massive amount of property in Charlottesville, Virginia back in 2007. Since then, the non-profit has spent $20 million on the effort to create "a mini-city" with a variety of building options. Even that amount of money can only be stretched so far, and they require a lot more in order to complete the ambitious project. They have turned to QOFs to support the effort and, down the road, intend to hand over building ownership to Charlottesville residents.

Some 2,800 miles away, in Gresham, Oregon, the Rockwood Community Development Corporation (RCDC), a non-profit serving low- and middle-income residents, created a for-profit B-corporation using QOFs intended to provide affordable housing. The B-corporation is investing in two ways: through a micro-cap limited partnership fund; and a real estate limited partnership.

A few major philanthropies, such as the Rockefeller Foundation, are investing substantial amounts of money in QOZs. In May 2019 the Foundation announced its plans to place $5.5 million in six cities with QOZ areas—the first being Newark, New Jersey—over a period of two years. The leaders of the Foundation are taking extensive precautions to ensure the money ends up in the right places, benefiting QOZ residents. The hope is that QOF investors and other foundations will follow suit and apply investment funds into QOZs.

The Kresge Foundation, based in Troy, Michigan, has been approaching QOZ support in a somewhat more conservative, but equally viable manner. Only five years shy of the centennial since it was founded, Kresge has already spent decades supporting communities with endowments, grants, and social investments. It is estimated that, by the end of 2019, it will offer $3.6 billion on endowments alone.

In March 2019, Kresge announced that it has invested $22 million to QOZ-related investments through Arctaris Impact and Community Capital Management, which are prepared to provide "transparency, accountability, and disclosure." The Foundation and fund managers are targeting a goal of over $800 million of investments in QOFs toward QOZs.

The Stanford Social Innovation Review suggests four proven ways that foundations can invest in QOFs through QOZs:

- **Support Independent Transaction Advisors:** Private and independent experts can identify investment areas suitable for your areas of interest and connect you with appropriate local officials in the QOZ.

- **Support Policy-Aligned Fund Managers:** Look for fund managers who are passionate about supporting QOZs.

- **Be Hyper-Local:** Target fund managers who are committed to specific communities and have insider's knowledge about them. It's easier to identify your strategic commonalities with such managers and then trust that they will share and protect your interests in helping the communities.

- **Develop and Track Success Metrics:** At this time, there aren't many reporting requirements for QOFs to investors. Foundations investing in these funds have a vested interest in setting up proper methods for monitoring and tracking progress and results. More likely than not, they will be proactive in setting up comprehensive metrics to evaluate reporting and data.

It's Time to Get Schooled

Education is an area that is near and dear to my heart. As someone who grew up without a proper education (although I compensated for this later on), I understand what it feels like to be behind the curve. Trust me when I say that investments in education QOFs will pay off richly for future generations in these communities.

I wholeheartedly agree with the quarterly journal *Education Next,* which cites opportunities encompassing a number of areas affiliated with improving education and believes they have the potential to span all age groups from early childhood right on up through college level. As you will see, they offer ideas peripheral but equally as relevant to classroom learning.

Early Childhood and After School Care
Families in distressed communities often struggle to find affordable childcare solutions. This becomes particularly challenging in scenarios involving single parents, two full-time working parents, or when one or both parents must take on more than one job in order to make ends meet.

Whether it's regarding nursery school, after school care, tutoring, or enrichment programs, QOFs can help in a number of different ways. *Education Next* also recommends investing in QOFs that offer new facilities or rehabilitate existing ones for providers. The journal goes on to offer the example of Dayton, Ohio, where investors are being offered the opportunity to help finance a new public library or an after school community center. Not only that, small business owners interested in starting professional tutoring centers may also obtain funding.

Elementary and Secondary Schools
Given all of the statistics presented in Part One, it shouldn't surprise you to learn that over 70% of students attending schools in QOZs are part of low-income families. The school systems in these areas suffer

from poor funding, which means they can't afford to hire the best teachers, properly maintain the facilities, and provide essential learning tools (such as books, computers, etc.). It goes without saying the school ratings in QOZs are lower than the national average.

Education Next reports a number of creative ideas for QOF investment suggested by the 21st Century School Fund (also known as 21CSF, an organization which is "...dedicated to building the public will and capacity to modernize public school facilities so they support high quality education and community revitalization"):

1. **Building Improvement:** Investors can partner with developers and the school district to form a public-private partnership. While the investors would technically "own" the buildings during the term and finance renovations and improvements, the districts retain sole control of them. Once the term ends, ownership reverts back to the school districts.

    In addition, investors could tap into QOFs to fulfill unmet community needs such as upgrading community centers, health facilities, childcare centers, and libraries. Many areas already have what is known as "community schools" to supplement flagging school systems; the same funds can be directed to improving these buildings.

    Why limit the imagination? It's also entirely possible to start all over again and build new schools in QOZs, which would breathe fresh life into the educational systems and assist students, teachers, and administrators alike.

    Greenpoint Landing, an area in Brooklyn, New York, is benefiting from investments that will revitalize the neighborhood: a new public school for preschoolers through eighth grade; 1,400 affordable apartments; and nine acres of parks.

2. **Teachers Villages:** Nineteenth century historian Henry Adams once said, "A teacher affects eternity; he can never tell where his influence stops." (Of course, Adams should have said "he *or she*," but that's an issue for another day...) Teachers deserve immeasurable respect for their tangible and intangible impact on our children. Unfortunately, as most of us are well aware, they often get the short end of the yardstick when

it comes to their salaries and benefits. As of this writing, the national average teacher salary in the U.S. is $58,000 per year; however, this is a grossly deceptive statistic, as thirty-six states fall below this number. This means that some states (such as New York, with an average teacher salary of over $79,000 per year) are well above the average and influence the overall number.

Imagine a single parent elementary schoolteacher with three children living in a QOZ. How does she even manage to afford rent in an apartment located anywhere near the school? Enter: *teacher villages*!

This idea of teachers villages has been around for a while. Some communities, such as California's Santa Clara Unified school district, recognized the issue and initiated a project that involved re-purposing local building space near schools to create affordable teacher housing.

In Newark, New Jersey, a developer named Ron Beit proposed a $150 million Teachers Village through his company, the RBH Group. The theory, supported once again by Cory Booker (whether you agree with his politics or not, you have to admit he is a very busy man!) is that casinos and sports teams don't build great communities—*great teachers do*. The Teachers Village not only offers affordable housing, but also surrounding perks such as a fitness center, a bakery, and salon. As you can imagine, luring remarkable teachers to this community improves *everything* in the surrounding area: the schools, the businesses, and the quality of life.

Not to mention the fact that Mr. Beit is a shrewd businessman and is *making money* on his noble investment. If you add in additional QOF support and investor savings in capital gains, the sky is the limit with everyone profiting at the same time.

3. **Charter Schools:** Most people think of a *desert* as a steaming hot and dry place with lots of sand, snakes, cacti, and tumbleweeds. Well, things are so bad for some school systems in QOZs that they have been dubbed *charter deserts*. While you have probably gleaned the meaning from the phrase alone, it specifically refers to stretches of land consisting of "three or more contiguous, moderate-to-high-poverty census tracts

without charter elementary schools." A whopping *70% of QOZs are charter deserts.* I need a glass of cold lemonade just thinking about it!

QOFs can play an important role in helping establish charter schools in QOZs or simply assist in financing them. In May 2019, for example, Starwood Capital Group announced a QOZ strategy in South Bronx, New York involving developer AB Capstone. The 147,000 square foot project features the Zeta Charter School as its centerpiece and even includes both retail and apartment units.

Lest you think that all of these efforts are only taking place in the northeast, let's head down south to Florida where, on a state-wide level, leaders, educators, and developers have created charter schools known as "Schools of Hope." In April 2019, Republican Florida Governor Ron DeSantis announced that he intends to expand the charter school effort "five-fold" through QOF funding in QOZs.

Colleges and Universities

People tend to think that all colleges and universities have deep pockets because of rich endowments, alumni support and, of course, exorbitant tuition costs. But this is not always the case, especially for institutions located in QOZs.

QOFs can assist higher education in a number of different ways, starting with improving research facilities, supporting technology, and helping to finance affordable local student housing. Statistics have proven that students who live on campus for two years have a 25% higher chance of graduating. They also have a significantly higher GPA coupled with an improved chance of making Dean's list.

An eye-opening statistic is that half of all Historically Black Colleges and Universities (HBCU) are situated in QOZs. (Note: The term Historically Black Colleges and Universities refers to institutions "established prior to 1964 with the intention of offering accredited, high-quality education to African American students across the United States.") Renaissance Equity Partners created a $50 million QOF to HBCUs in order to help students obtain affordable on-campus housing, among other important purposes.

I wholeheartedly recommend that investors pay a great deal of attention to colleges and universities located in QOZs. Not only can they help further the education of people of lesser means and house them, they can use QOFs to create all kinds of beneficial programs, such as entrepreneurship incubators (which we will cover later on). The QOFs could help subsidize worthwhile entrepreneurial ventures with both building facilities and startup capital, offering a major leg-up in the business world for students. Most colleges and universities have active alumni programs, which are an excellent source for potential QOF partnerships.

Class dismissed—at least until our next area of community focus: infrastructure.

Structure a QOF on Infrastructure

Throughout this book I've provided a number of examples of communities with crumbling infrastructure. In April 2019, the Economic Development Association (EDA) actually started doing something about it. Where? You guessed it—in QOZs!

Whoever said infrastructure isn't sexy for investors is in for quite an awakening. The EDA, which has already invested $13 million on twenty-two projects in QOZs since 2018, offers fine examples of how to allocate QOF funds into helping repair community infrastructure. The goal all along has been not only to lend direct assistance to QOZs, but also to encourage other investors to follow the organization's lead and (as it were) flood money into those areas.

Specifically, the EDA provided a $2.5 million grant in Dubuque, Iowa to replace flood infrastructure and safeguard local businesses. Elsewhere, in Durant, Oklahoma, the EDA invested $1.5 million in water infrastructure improvements designed to support business growth in the area. In addition to creating numerous jobs, the efforts in Durant are anticipated to spark an additional $12 million from private QOF investors.

When seeking to invest in QOZs through QOFs, consider for one moment the many areas infrastructure entails:

- **Communications:** telephone cables and mobile phone towers.

- **Energy facilities:** power stations, power grids, power lines, wind farms, hydroelectric plants, etc.

- **Hubs:** ports, airports, waterways, and canals.

- **Land and property protection:** safeguards from floods resulting from hurricanes, tornados, etc.

- **Local safety:** police departments, prisons, and fire departments.

- **Sanitation:** waste removal and sanitation facilities.

- **Transportation:** roads, railways, tunnels, bridges, and mass-transit (such as buses and subways).

- **Water sources:** reservoirs, dams, pumping stations, and levees.

The Global Resilience Institute at Northeastern University has published a series of blogs demonstrating just how "resilient" QOFs can be in handling a wide variety of infrastructure issues in QOZs—both prevention and resolving mishaps (acts of God and human negligence or error). Aging gas lines, hurricane electricity outages, wildfire recovery, and dam leakage are just a few of the subjects covered by these fascinating blogs.

As mentioned in earlier chapters, communities can suffer potentially tragic losses in lives, property, land, and businesses when their infrastructure fails. You can select specific areas of infrastructure in the QOZs of your choosing to invest in and help prevent such damage before it can occur.

That said, disaster prevention does not need to be the sole area of focus for infrastructure improvement and repair. What about maintaining a community's parks and landmarks? The condition of a local park speaks volumes about the pride the community takes in itself. If, for example, the irrigation system in a community park is faulty, the plants, flowers, and trees will wither, and the area won't serve as an attractive destination for residents and tourists. In addition, if there aren't working street lamps in a local park, would visitors feel safe enough to take evening strolls through it?

On the other hand, if a park has lush greens, blossoming flowers, statues commemorating its local heroes, comfortable benches, functioning street lamps, and free concerts and events, the picture starts to look a lot rosier. QOF investments can play a major role in helping to revitalize these parks and make them a more beautiful, exciting, and safer place for people to commune.

In order to get involved in park creation or upgrades—or any infrastructure improvement, for that matter—a great place to start is contacting an organization such as the EDA or to simply approach the community's chamber of commerce. These organizations would most likely be thrilled to help you pinpoint where the most desperate assistance is needed.

Ganging up on Gangs

We've already explored how QOF investments can help improve schools and community centers, which would no doubt have a positive impact on reducing youth-related crime and involvement in drugs, as well as discouraging interest in gang involvement. As it happens, the U.S. government had the foresight to consider how QOZ status could be used to directly deter gang-related crime and violence. Who knew the government was capable of such presence of mind?

In April 2019, the OJJDP—which, by the way, stands for the Office of Juvenile Justice and Delinquency Prevention—released a massive "Competitive Grant Solicitation" as an anticipated benefit of TCJA and QOZ legislation. The solicitation invites communities suffering from high volume of gang activity to apply for grants (maximum of $320,000 for each application) intended to support victims of gang violence, as well as deter crime in general. I consider it a ripe opportunity for investors to take advantage of supplementing the funding for this wide-ranging and important government initiative.

QOFs Can Help Support Health Care

It shouldn't be the least bit surprising that one third of QOZs have a hospital situated in the zones or within a half mile nearby. The combination of drugs and crime on the rise in most QOZs—along with the ballooning costs of health care—are cause for serious alarm. Urban and rural QOZ communities across the country struggle to cover the needs of their residents, both young and old.

Not only can investing in QOFs located in QOZs raise the standards of hospital and medical care—in terms of the buildings, the equipment, the medical staff, the research capabilities, and so much more—they can offer greater availability of critical treatments, improve health education and awareness, and even prevent illness. It often goes unnoticed that hospitals are the biggest employers in their areas—as well as substantial holders of real estate property—and, for those reasons alone, they are worth their weight in QOF investment dollars.

While researching this book, I found it enlightening to discover how active many hospitals are in terms of helping communities in areas that are tangential to their services. They address everything from drug intervention and family support; to nursing care programs; to homelessness and assisted living; to food banks; and on and on.

Hospitals can achieve even more with QOF investments. By partnering with hospitals, your capital can have virtually unlimited impact in distressed areas because of the extensive nature of hospital affiliations.

Policymap.com recommends that hospitals develop the following to make QOF investing in them even easier and more inviting: a community health prospectus; capital stacks to support the investment prospectus; and a plan to serve as a local clearinghouse of strong investments.

So, What Are You Waiting For?

As I indicated, this chapter serves as just a teeny-tiny glimpse into what QOFs can do to re-energize communities. For all of the QOZ areas vested in their futures—such as Youngstown, Ohio—QOFs can offer a sense of renewed hope and potential for things to finally turn around and get better. Non-profits, education, infrastructure, gang violence, and health care are a mere sliver of the myriad areas that may be improved by QOFs.

Are you impressed yet? If the answer is *yes*, start mapping out your QOF strategy in QOZs right now! These deserving urban and rural communities can't wait another minute for you to hop aboard and start making a difference.

For our next stop, we are going to change tracks and learn how to make a difference from an entirely new perspective. Bear with me on this; I promise we won't venture off the rails.

In Chapter Seven, rather than continuing to see things from primarily the investor's point of view, we will place ourselves inside the shoes of a business owner situated in a QOZ. The plight of this individual is unique, and therefore it is well worth the time for all readers to get immersed in it, whether you happen to be this person or not. Once I've painted a picture of the business owner's circumstances in a QOZ, I will offer specifics on how he or she can partner with QOF investors to improve the existing business.

All aboard! The next train is heading non-stop to the business owner in a QOZ.

CHAPTER SEVEN

IMPROVING MY COMPANY IN A QOZ

Our train has arrived at the station. Which one? Take your pick of any of the nearly 8,800 rural or urban QOZ areas.

Next, let's hop on whichever mode of transportation is available in this QOZ and strikes your fancy: subway, bus, Uber, or rental car (if you happen to want to spend some time and become familiar with the area).

Where are we headed? To the establishment of a larger-sized business located in the QOZ. Feel free to use your imagination about what type of business it is, the products/services it offers, and whom it serves. For the moment, none of that specificity matters. Use your imagination and select any industry you like: manufacturing, warehousing, brick-and-mortar retail, professional services—you name it.

Once there, what is the first thing you notice about the neighborhood? Maybe the blocks surrounding the business are a bit rundown. A couple of storefronts are boarded up. You feel a touch of sadness, knowing the town's rich history and that at one time it had been a thriving business community.

When you reach your destination—the company you conjured in your head—what is your initial impression? Is the company sign out front a bit slanted?

Once inside the big building, do you notice that the carpet is stained and frayed and the walls seemingly unpainted in years? If there is an elevator going up, does it sound creaky and overdue for an inspection?

You enter the main reception area. The person greeting you says one of the owners has been expecting you. As she leads you to her boss's office, you pass by a few abandoned workstations amidst the ones that are filled with dedicated employees.

Sally Ryan, a senior executive and one of the business owners, welcomes you into her office. She is polite, professional, and enthusiastic about her work, but seems unable to conceal the fact that she is anxious and distracted. You don't have to be Sherlock Holmes to deduce that times have been tough for Sally and the business. She has been struggling for quite some time going all the way back to the recession, from which the business and her community have never fully recovered.

It's time to close your eyes and imagine you are slipping into Sally's shoes. (If you happen to be a gentleman, you can visualize that they don't have heels. This is pretend, after all.) What do you suppose is foremost on her mind?

How are we going to pay our bills?

How can we reduce costs?

How can we boost revenue?

Will we have to reduce salaries?

Will we have to lay off even more people?

How much longer will the business be able to stay afloat—we're barely treading water as it is.

Maybe we should relocate to a big town with a flourishing economy. Our costs will increase, but at least we'll have some chance of scaling back up.

But wait. So many other businesses have left in droves already. They've taken their families with them. It's becoming a ghost town here. If we move, we're giving up on a community that we've worked so hard to support over many decades. Deep down I love this place and care about my neighbors. What will happen if other businesses follow our lead? What will be left? What will happen to the streets, the schools, the parks, and everything else?

Sally, her co-owners, and her management team indeed have a conundrum. They understand the ripple effect of what happens to the entire community when one business abandons ship...and then another...and another.

Does it have to end this way? *No.* Is there anything she and her business partners and associates can do about it? *Yes and yes.*

Saving Sally Ryan

In the previous chapters, we looked at businesses in QOZs from the outside. Now we are looking at them from within. Certainly, it is possible for investors to choose to invest in QOFs based on their investment objectives that will help Sally and her co-business owners. However, this presumes they already know about the QOZ provision and are in the process of searching for opportunities in her area.

But let's say you happen *to be* Sally (or a Harry) and you just discovered that your business is located in an approved QOZ. Bingo! You've leapt over the first hurdle. You feel a glimmer of hope that there is a way the business can remain in the community and become revitalized. Where and how do you start to find a QOF that will invest in your business?

Step One: Passing the Test

Remember when I told you about all of the various "tests"—the *original use* test, the *substantial improvement* test, et. al.—back in Chapter Five? Well, you can relax and take a deep breath. I'm not going to test you on all of that!

The main thing you must know for a QOF to invest in your business— or for the business to create a QOF for itself, which is far more challenging for reasons detailed below—is *that the transaction must pass the original use test or the substantial improvement test.* Without getting into all of that gobbledygook all over again, here is a condensed refresher:

- *Original use* test: The property cannot have been built and served a source of revenue before the time the QOF was created.

Or:

- *Substantial improvement* test: In order for the QOF to qualify, the improvements done after the transaction must be equal or greater than the purchase.

As you can see, these tests make it difficult—though not impossible— to create a QOF for your own business. The *original use* test is hard for an existing business to overcome because the company evidently had at least *some* value before the QOF was created. The alternative, the substantial improvement test, means you need to fund the overhaul with the equivalent value of the business earnings. If you already have this amount to begin with, it's unlikely you are in a position that necessitates creating the QOF in the first place.

Let's presume you are seeking an outside QOF to revitalize your business and have passed one of the aforementioned tests. You are ready to move on to the next step.

Step Two: Attracting QOF Investors

If your home is up for sale and you are about to have an open house, you rearrange furniture, organize your stuff, tidy up, and bake some aromatic bread to make a favorable impression to realtors and potential buyers. Readying your business to lure QOF investors isn't all that different from this scenario. In fact, it's not much of a departure from luring in investors for regular investments that have nothing to do with QOZ legislation.

Yes, QOF investors are presumably on the hunt for QOZ businesses in order to take advantage of all of the benefits, but don't take anything for granted. Being a business in need within a QOZ doesn't automatically mean investors are bursting through your front door. You are competing against thousands of other QOZ businesses, so you need to get everything in order and ensure your business is at its best. In other words, your company must appear to be "investment ready" with a bright future. Perhaps it just needs a little investment boost in the right direction.

Some points for investment readiness to take into consideration as you search for prospects:

1. Is your business a low-risk/high-return proposition?
2. Does your business have a proven past track record? Although your business may not be where it should be at the moment, you still need to demonstrate that it has had strong performance over the years. In other words, the past must intersect with the future (see #4).
3. Have you done everything possible to reduce costs: streamline processes, cut back capital expenses, etc.?
4. Have you created a Five- or Ten-Year Plan to demonstrate where your business is headed? Investors are paying for future anticipated earnings.
5. Have you created a business strategy to support and implement the Five- or Ten-Year Plan?
6. Have you outlined all of the things a QOF investment can accomplish to improve the business and increase revenue and profit?

7. Have you demonstrated where your industry stands and why it is poised for growth?
8. Have you laid out your company's USP (Unique Selling Proposition) that makes it stand out against the competition?
9. Are your business finances organized, transparent, and well presented?
10. How strong is your leadership team?
11. How solid is your workforce? What special talents, expertise, and local knowledge do they have?

Step Three: Gift Wrap Your QOZ Business

Earlier in this book I touched on the idea of "telling a story" about your business. A "good story" is where you briefly set your business apart from all of the others and command attention. This step is where you must become a magical (but truth-telling) narrator, conveying a bit of engaging company history while demonstrating what makes it special. The more energy, enthusiasm, and excitement you apply to your story, the greater impact it will have.

Think of it like an elevator pitch. Conciseness and passion are key. If you were only to have sixty seconds in an elevator with a QOF investor, what story would you tell about your business? Certainly, any details that might appeal to emotion would be welcome. For example (don't feel the need to cover all of these areas—keep it brief!):

- *Who founded your company?* What if this individual was a bootstrapping immigrant who came to this country with nothing except the clothes he wore and a nickel in his pocket?

- *When was your company founded?* If the business has been around since World War II and pitched in with resources for that effort, this tidbit would be interesting and inspirational to include.

- *Has your company played a greater role in the community?* Perhaps your company sponsored a memorial near town hall in honor of those lost in 9/11. An organization that cares will appeal on an emotional level to some investors.

- *How did your company weather economic storms?* Maybe your business shifted gears during the recession and created a lower-cost product your customers could better afford in difficult times. Nimbleness, scrappiness, adaptability, and survival instincts are attractive traits in a company striving for success.

All of the above would be excellent "gift wrapping" options in helping your company look sexy for QOF investors. The trick is to identify the best story for *your* company. You must look at the organization from an outside perspective: not just to rectify solvable problems, but also to accentuate the hidden gold within it. Sometimes the people within a company are too close to the details to see what gems are hidden in plain sight.

Another point that should not be taken for granted: Since there is a ten-year requirement for QOF investors to benefit from capital gains savings, anything you can do to demonstrate a company lifespan of a decade or more would be advantageous.

Invite Everyone to the QOF Party

While it might be tempting to put a lid on your QOF investment outreach to avoid attracting additional "competition," there is much greater benefit to widening the net and including other businesses in the effort. If another local business is successful, it helps the greater good of community improvement. Down the road, this will greatly benefit your business as well.

Other business owners and community leaders may not know about QOZ legislation in the TCJA. Or, perhaps they don't understand what it is and how it can be beneficial. This is where you come in and help spread the message. Rally local business owners and community leaders and share all of your QOZ educational wisdom with them. (Don't forget, I already gave you a degree on this in an earlier chapter!) Brainstorm with them to identify what kinds of community investments they would want to see. Next, make sure they conform to aforementioned QOZ regulations.

Several businesses will join the QOF party right away; others may be shy at first, but will become more social once they see the large crowd of people who are already enthusiastically involved.

Meanwhile, the eyes of community leaders bug out when they realize how QOF investments can benefit an infinite number of areas. As

I mentioned in the previous chapter, QOFs can invest in education, infrastructure, beautification projects, hospitals, housing, community centers, and so many other things. The leaders need to get together and prioritize which ones are of the greatest urgency, as well as those that might be the most attractive to QOF investors.

Dear readers: That is merely the beginning of the effort! Awareness should spread everywhere in the community. Anyone could—and *should*—get involved. These are just a few things citizens can do to pitch in to help the cause and lure QOF investors:

1. Create pamphlets about the identified community projects and the potential impact of QOZ legislation.
2. Distribute the pamphlets door-to-door and keep stacks in public places: libraries, town halls, grocery stores, drugstores, storefronts, etc.
3. Call a town hall meeting to introduce the proposed plans for luring QOZ investors.
4. As mentioned earlier in this book, some QOZs have already included information about the tax law and its benefits on their community websites. You can approach the administrators of the community's website (which may be the chamber of commerce, town council, or some other organizational body) and propose they add a tab with descriptive content that invites QOFs for local businesses and community projects such as your own.

Regarding number four: Alas, as with most things, there may be some politics or bureaucracy involved in getting changes approved and implemented on the website by the powers that be. If you hit a brick wall, don't let that stop you! (We will cover this extensively in Chapter Fifteen.) You can take measures into your own hands by creating your own QOZ website. Of course, you can partner with other businesses in the area—even competitors (again, there is nothing whatsoever wrong with this, you are all in it together!)—and ask them to pitch in. The website would:

- Identify all of the local QOZ areas.

- Explain the applicable portions of the TCJA.

- Highlight the previously explained benefits of investing in QOFs located in QOZs.

- Present the many wonderful types of businesses in your community.

- Emphasize community projects that have been prioritized for revitalization.

- Demonstrate that the businesses are fully vested in improving themselves and their communities.

- Post success stories with pictures: community revitalization projects, businesses that have expanded, and so forth.

I hope you've enjoyed traveling to the QOZ, putting yourself in Sally's shoes, and involving other businesses in the effort. If you follow the instructions in this chapter and join together with other business owners, executives, civic leaders, and fellow citizens, your business will grow and profit; the area will revitalize and blossom; and the entire business and public community will feel a renewed sense of pride in itself and find renewed hope for the future.

PART FOUR

RUNNING A PROFITABLE QOF

CHAPTER EIGHT

CHOOSING THE RIGHT INDUSTRY AND COMPANY

Right about now I imagine that your head is bursting with excitement at the thought of the many possibilities available in QOZs. You have a solid understanding of legislation and guidelines; know what QOFs can accomplish for QOZ businesses, communities, and your own top-line and bottom-line through capital gains savings; and can even see the perspective from the QOZ business owner (or you may be one yourself).

In this part of the book, we'll take this accumulated knowledge one step further. I'll guide you through the essentials of how to jumpstart a profitable QOF, beginning with selecting an appropriate industry and identifying the company that best fits your business strategy and, hopefully, inspires you as well.

It's Okay to Play to Your Areas of Strength

If your investment strategy is to focus on specific areas of business, such as commercial real estate or technology, there is no reason for you to switch gears in the case of QOFs. You will no doubt be able to mine your power alleys in QOZs. In fact, if you feel any reservations whatsoever about QOZ businesses, staying in your industry comfort zone is probably a wise idea. You may have some invaluable knowledge from your years of experience to pass along that could be beneficial to turning these businesses from the red into the black.

It goes without saying that having passion for a specific industry can go a long way toward building trust with QOZ business owners and establishing a shared bond that would offset the possibility of them believing you have an ulterior motive. They will relate to your passion and therefore may work even harder to help you meet your strategic investment goals.

Lastly, at the risk of repeating myself, QOFs are not quick business flips. You are in it for the long haul: up to ten years, to be precise, in order to capitalize on the capital gains advantages. Having an affinity for a particular investment area means you'll understand its peaks and valleys and that you'll be patient with it for the duration. The QOZ businesses will appreciate your commitment to ensuring their long-term success.

There is also less chance you'll get bored with it and have an itch to move on to something else. Ten years can feel like a long time—but it's a snap of the fingers in an investment cycle.

While on the hunt for the right QOZ, do some preliminary research to see where your preferred area of industry happens to be thriving—or, at least, is showing positive signs of improvement.

Apply Business Savvy, Common Sense, and a Dash of Sensitivity

I'm sure that, as a wise investor, you know all the ins and outs and have sound business strategies for identifying opportunities and trends in your preferred industry (or industries). QOZs are something of a different kettle of fish, however. What works in thriving cities may not apply to distressed rural communities (and vice versa) due to cultural differences or simply because the areas simply haven't caught up to the trend yet—or have lacked the advantages to make it work.

For example, an upscale coffee bar may work just fine in a growing city, but it's probably not such a great idea in a QOZ out of the starting gate. If the area is distressed, it's unlikely its citizens and workers are prepared to shell out $4+ on a fancy cup of coffee. On the other hand, a coffee truck offering a cup of Joe for $1 that is placed near a QOZ business under construction or that is being remodeled sounds like an excellent idea to me, as it's affordably priced and would fill the morning caffeine (and sugar) needs of site workers.

I am not going to get on a high horse preaching about the rights and wrongs of certain kinds of investing. But I will point out one direction that strikes me as going against the grain of the intent of the QOZ initiative: investments that inflate the cost of living at the expense of current residents.

Let's examine this more closely. On the surface, a deluxe residential apartment complex in a QOZ to house executives and professionals sounds like a promising idea. The QOF investors and developers of the project are thrilled at the prospect of gutting a decaying old building and converting it into state of the art apartments, for which they can charge quintuple the rent.

But ask yourself the following questions: What happens to the current residents? Do they have to relocate to an even more distressed town because they can't afford the rent hike? Or, in the case of newly constructed upscale apartments, will that raise the cost of living for the low-income residents of the community who have been scraping for years just to get by?

This backlash scenario would be a harsh irony, to say the least, considering the QOZ legislation in the TCJA is intended *to help* communities and their citizens. Investors and developers who bulldoze through QOZs may see lush opportunity, which is wonderful—but we don't wish to see that happen at the expense of good people. No matter how inadvertent, this direction would be completely contrary to the intent of the QOZ initiative. Clearly, some sensitivity and sound judgment are required.

As of this writing, the government has not provided a safety net for this. (Nor do I necessarily think it makes sense to create regulations of this sort that might de-incentivize investors and developers). I agree with Eddie Lorin, founder of Strategic Realty Holdings and a member of the Opportunity Zones Coalition, who wrote: "It is my opinion that the onus…will eventually fall on developers and investors themselves… to ensure that their investor dollars work to improve area conditions for *existing* residents—not to replace them entirely with wealthier ones."

The upshot is this: I want you to make money and for the community— the *entire* community, that is—to reap the benefits. If residential real estate is the central focus of your investment strategy, that's fine. Before mapping out plans with marble floors and golden staircases, however, take into consideration whether or not this benefits or harms the current residents of this particular community. It may draw in an affluent population, but at the same time uproot many more hard-working Americans.

Instead, consider an option that involves radically improving an existing residential building or creating a beautiful new one from scratch—and *making it affordable.* You will still make money on the investment as well as save on capital gains. This is far better than forcing people to move from one distressed community and into another one that is probably even worse, don't you think? At a later date, once the current residences have been restored and the community has begun to flourish, then you can create the golden luxury skyscrapers of your dreams.

Following the Lead of Erie, PA

There is one community in particular that has already recognized and embraced QOZ legislation: Erie, Pennsylvania. This historic city, located on Lake Erie, was first settled by Europeans (the French, who created Fort Presque Isle and remained only temporarily) in 1753 and incorporated in 1851. In the Battle of Lake Erie during the War of 1812, Commodore Oliver Perry led a major victory over the British fleet. Over the years, the city became known as a major hub for fishing, shipbuilding, and commerce, and later as a major manufacturing center. It earned the All America City Award in 1972.

Like parts of Philadelphia, Allentown, and several other vital Pennsylvania cities, Erie fell on hard times due to the recession, shifts in manufacturing, and other factors. It recently experienced a distressed score of over 98% with a 56% unemployment rate and a 43% poverty rate. But, thanks to QOZ legislation and strong business leadership led by John Persinger, CEO of Erie Downtown Development Corporation, they are working hard to reverse the trend via creative projects backed by QOF investments. They are attempting to establish a brand new, welcoming ecosystem to encourage startups and entrepreneurship in the downtown area. Among some of the initiatives already in progress:

- The Flagship Opportunity Zone Corporation has developed an investment portfolio of fourteen projects and businesses with more in the works.

- Erie Insurance—the city's largest employer—has created a $50 million QOF to support a food hall and market that will form a brand new culinary arts district. The project will feature apartments, provide space for twenty businesses, and employ nearly 250 people.

- CapZone Impact Investments and the Erie Innovation District have partnered to create a $10 million QOF focused on IT and cyber-security startups through the Secure Erie Accelerator.

(You'll learn more about accelerators later on in this chapter.)

- The Erie Innovation District organized a smart city program to implement WiFi, LED lighting, and security cameras throughout Erie QOZs.

The above just offers a taste of what a business community can accomplish by understanding QOZ benefits, tapping into the right business leadership, and establishing some creative partnerships. The last bullet is particularly impressive, as the technical improvements and additions make the district much more inviting to new businesses. Not only will investors, leaders, entrepreneurs, staff, and workers have better connectivity to run their businesses more efficiently, their partners, vendors, and customers will have plenty of bars on their phones when visiting the area. In addition, the lighting and security cameras will diffuse any fears anyone might have had about personal safety in the district. In other words, Erie, PA has sent a clear-cut message to businesses that they are ready, willing, and able to sustain QOFs.

Now it's time for us to get even more granular with all of the industries that have potential for benefiting from QOF investments. When it comes right down to it, there is no limitation on the many possibilities—but I am going to lay many of them out anyway to spark your imagination.

Getting Real with Real Estate

Real estate—both residential and commercial—are rather obvious avenues for investing in QOZs, so let's spend some time reviewing the *not-so-obvious* types of buildings where QOFs can make a difference.

Taking Up Residence
In terms of residential homes, you can certainly invest in a traditional apartment complex with a full service gross lease. You can also establish a QOF for condominiums or town houses with a full service gross lease. An even more exciting proposition would be to offer opportunities that enable multi-family QOZ residents to eventually purchase and own their own homes at reasonable prices.

Hotels and Motels

The standard of living in a community is often judged by the quality of its hotels and motels, so this is a wonderful place to start. If tourists, investors, and business professionals happen to travel to the area, they don't want to spend their nights sleeping in grungy establishments. A good hotel in a convenient and safe area with clean, comfortable rooms and excellent service can make the difference to spark repeat tourism and increase investments in the area.

Hotels may also potentially offer additional value within the property: a bar; a restaurant; an exercise facility; a gift shop; a business center; conference rooms; catering halls; and private meeting space. These days, many hotels are located within shopping malls—or the other way around—for extra convenience to visitors.

On the Hunt for Hospitality

But why be limited to the plain concept of a traditional hotel or motel? Hospitality businesses come in numerous forms. In certain communities, it might make some sense to create a cozy thematic lodge or bed and breakfast. For example, in a rural area known for its rivers, streams, and woods, you could build a flyfishing or hunting lodge. When it comes to QOZs, consider the history and culture of the community—but with an eye toward the future.

There's Always Space for Retail Space

It is no secret that online shopping and digitization have become extremely popular and, in some cases, have made certain types of brick-and-mortar businesses obsolete. (Hint: Try finding a movie rental store nowadays.) But this doesn't mean that many people still don't enjoy the notion of browsing shops and physically touching and trying on items before purchasing them. For example, I suspect that anyone looking to adopt a kitten or puppy would much rather touch, hold, and get to personally know the animal at a pet shop or shelter rather than "ordering" such a beloved future family member online.

Try as Starbucks might, you still can't order a tall coffee electronically and have a steaming cup delivered through your mobile phone. (Drone delivery for coffee also doesn't seem like such a good idea; I envision it being deposited right over a customer's head!) Coffee shops (not too upscale, mind you) are, therefore, a good real estate investment. Even better, for a real treat, why not an ice cream or frozen yogurt shop or a candy store?

In fact, anything in the food service industry can potentially be a lucrative QOF investment: restaurants, donut shops, grocery stores, delis, bakeries, and so forth.

If you are a fan of words such as *vegan, gluten-free,* and *all natural,* how about retail space for a vitamin shop, a fruit/vegetable stand, or an organic food store? These types of businesses seem to be sprouting up everywhere! (Please forgive me for that one...)

Next we come to the types of products that people must try on or test out before making the actual purchase. Or, consumers *must have* the items right away. Impulse purchases are great for brick-and-mortar retail stores that supply items people don't want to wait for—even if it could be sent via overnight delivery or drone. While it is possible to purchase sneakers and shoes online (often more cheaply), there is still great demand to open a box, slide on the fresh footwear, and take the pair out for a test drive stroll on store carpeting. There is still no substitute for a knowledgeable salesperson who knows the latest styles and can help you find just the right look and fit.

This can be equally as true when it comes to clothing, accessories, jewelry, and other fashion, which is where boutique shops come in. It goes without saying that the nicer you make the storefront, the more inviting it will be. If there are dozens of such shops in one area, then it becomes a destination for tourists and the like and improves the QOZ community as a whole.

Places for Production and Fulfillment
No matter how many physical retail stores end up being overtaken by online businesses, the need for real estate space to create products and house them has never been greater. Buildings for manufacturing, assembly, processing, shipping, warehousing, and storage can be solid QOF investments.

These facilities would also spur excellent employment opportunities in the QOZ. Even the most high tech, automated plant requires a workforce to feed, operate, clean, and maintain the machinery and ensure quality control.

Servicing the Needs

When it comes to service, *immediate needs* often come into play. If something in your home or business is broken, you need or want to get it fixed right away. You don't want to wait several days or weeks for your laptop to be shipped out, repaired, and then sent back—so a local computer/electronics repair shop might prove invaluable. In some cases, such as lawn mower, bicycle, and car repair shops, you couldn't ship those things out for repair even if you wanted to.

Taking Office—Space, That Is

Although many companies have now gone the "virtual" route with off-site employees, there is still ample opportunity to create professional office building space with full gross leases that need a physical location in order to serve the needs of the community. Accounting and law firms rank high on this list, as do health care professionals such as dentists, chiropractors, cardiologists, physical therapists, orthopedists, gynecologists, urologists, psychologists/counselors/psychiatrists, optometrists, and so forth.

While we are on the subject of health care, a twenty-four hour emergency clinic centrally located in the QOZ would also be a beneficial idea. Other ideas for centers include: drug intervention and family support centers; nursing care programs; shelters and assisted living facilities; food banks; etcetera.

Buildings Can Be for Fun, Too

Every rural and urban community needs inviting and safe recreational places to entertain people of all ages. If a QOZ doesn't have boys and girls clubs, daycare centers, and senior centers, you might want the QOF to fund them. But why stop there? How about considering one of these ideas:

- Amphitheaters.

- Amusement Parks.

- Aquariums.

- Arenas.

- Bowling Alleys.

- Concert Centers.

- Conference, Expo, and Convention Centers.

- Equestrian Centers.

- Event Complexes.

- Fairgrounds.

- Gaming Facilities (where legal, of course).

- Golf Courses.

- Health and Fitness Centers.

- Mega Sportsplexes.

- Motorsport Tracks and Facilities.

- Movie Theaters.

- Performing Arts Centers.

- Skating Rinks.

- Ski Resorts.

- Sports Stadiums (including Little League and soccer fields).

- Waterpark Resorts.

As you have deduced by now, there are so many real estate options in QOZs that it is impossible to cover them all in one chapter. Once you've determined the community needs and the lot availability in the QOZ, the opportunities will sparkle right in front of your eyes.

Top Investment Sectors

Warren Buffett once famously said, "The best thing that happens to us is when a great company gets into temporary trouble.... We want to buy them when they're on the operating table."

There is quite a bit of truth to this statement from an investor's perspective. In a sense it's a variation of the cliché "Buy low, sell high." While this is a smart philosophy, you should also pay attention to the hottest industry trends when searching for investment bargains—especially those that are likely to have staying power. At present, these five areas show all signs that they will be at the forefront for a while:

- Energy, such as wind and solar power.

- Health Care, such as pharmaceuticals.

- Industrials, such as waste management.

- Technology, such as cybersecurity.

- Telecommunications, such as social media sites.

Again, it's fine to stay within your investment strategy and comfort zone. But also pay attention to the trends as well and see if there is room for you to stretch. It's entirely possible that a hot trend—such as wind and solar energy—hasn't had the chance to reach a particular QOZ, which means you could have an opportunity to be in on the ground floor with an investment in a QOF.

Digging Deep to Help the Community

If you are looking for long-term investments that will have unequivocally positive implications in the QOZ, look no further than educational institutions (everything from nursery schools to universities), non-profits (such as cancer research), and infrastructure (communications, energy facilities, hubs, land/property protection, public safety, sanitation, transportation, water sources, etc.). The QOZs will experience direct benefits from improvements in these areas, as people will be eager to flock to neighborhoods that provide good schools, clean water, and convenient modes of transportation. Many of the initiatives take several years to complete, which works just fine with regard to the long-term requirements for capital gains savings.

Going Out of the Box with Incubators and Accelerators

You may be thinking that the improvements necessary to turn some QOZs around might be too daunting for QOF investors to handle alone. In some cases, you aren't far off base, especially if you happen to be starting a fund from scratch. This is when some creative thinking comes into play to help develop concepts and grow existing businesses without feeling like you are "going it alone."

The following types of organizations can help you narrow down options for QOF investments and ramp up the process, since they are solely intended to help jump-start business ventures: *incubators* and *accelerators*. These sound like terms you might have heard back in biology class, so I'll separate them out and explain them in simple terms.

Business Incubators

According to Entrepreneur.com, these are organizations that are "designed to accelerate the growth and success of entrepreneurial companies through an array of business support resources and services that could include physical space, capital, coaching, common services, and networking connections."

Let's unwind that ball of yarn. Maybe you think way back to your grade school science class when the teacher brought in a tank full of chick eggs waiting to be hatched. The tank had to establish an appropriate environment heated to the right temperature in order for the goopy, feathery tykes to feel comfortable enough to poke their beaks through their shells and be welcomed into our dangerous world. If the temperature or some other element in the environment wasn't just right, the chick came out stillborn or didn't survive very long. This is a fragile time of life, indeed!

It's not that different for a fledgling startup entering the business community—goop and all. The new business requires just the right conditions and nurturing in order to survive and thrive. This is where the incubator comes in, establishing a safe and friendly place for the entity to take shape and be born right up until it can take its first full steps on its own.

The roles in an incubator can sometimes be confusing, so let's put it this way: Investors supply the "what" (meaning money), while the incubators more often than not provide the "where" (and sometimes the "who" as well). If a QOZ already has an established incubator location, working spaces may already exist that can serve as a platform for luring in partners, developers, and staff. In a sense, the incubators can serve as facilitators who have the ability to bring interested disparate entities together to ensure a project comes to fruition. They are also in a prime position to explain the specific needs and culture of the local community to outside parties.

Some business schools, such as Drexel University in Philadelphia, are at the forefront of business incubators. They established the Nowak Metro Finance Lab at Drexel and Accelerator for America to create tools, analyses, systems, and processes that can be replicated from one QOZ to the next. Think of all the time savings this program can enable! Why should QOZs and their investors have to reinvent the wheel if another entity has already mapped out the process? Think of it in terms of "idea sharing" or "instructor manuals" on how to replicate business models for QOFs in QOZs.

These are just a few of the invaluable tools that have already been made available through the Nowak Metro Finance Lab at Drexel and Accelerator for America:

- *Zone Typologies*: The lab has sifted through the nearly 8,800 QOZs to drill down into specific demographics and guide investors through finding the right location based on their strategies and interests. Data is divided into twenty- to twenty-five geographies that share various economic and social characteristics (such as types of commercial districts).

- *Deal Prototypes and Playbooks*: These guides explain different start-up methods and show how communities can work with investors to bring them to fruition.

- *Deal Books:* Known as the new "capital stacks," deal books explain legal ways to finance investments (housing, real estate, and many others).

- *Shared Equity Models:* These are to ensure that the benefits of the

QOFs return to the residents and businesses of the communities. Cornell Professor Joe Margulies proposed a concept known as a "Community Trust" to help distressed communities have some measure of control with regard to how resources are allocated.

- *City Cases*: In some cases, local institutions have the means to help QOZ businesses, but their bureaucracies are too complex or time-consuming to figure out. City Cases provide examples of how government offices have helped community growth in their areas that are translatable to other businesses.

Incubators, which are sometimes referred to as "startup collectives," may also come in the form of "coworking space"—which refers to the sharing of best practices within the community. They may hold seminars, offer resources, or share materials (such as the aforementioned Drexel Lab) to help launch and effectively run a business.

Business Accelerators

Smallbiztrends.com defines business accelerators as "…organizations that offer a range of support services and funding opportunities for startups. They tend to work by enrolling startups in months-long programs that offer mentorship, office space and supply chain resources. More importantly, business accelerator programs offer access to capital and investment in return for startup equity. Startups essentially 'graduate' from their accelerator program after three or four months—which means that development projects are time-sensitive and very intensive."

Now for the translation: Accelerators usually pick up from where the incubators left off. Whereas the latter helps create the environment to introduce the business concept to the world, the former facilitates the speed of its growth. Accelerators, which usually last between three to six months, offer specific tactical business advice to help businesses get through any roadblocks that are blocking or slowing down success. They can help with granular issues (such as finding a low-cost vendor for supplies) or major problems (such as managing debt or obtaining investment money).

So Many Other Options...

Yes, there are more—*many more*—ways to jumpstart a QOF. Some companies, such as Accenture (in Detroit, MI) and Steelcase (in Grand Rapids, MI), offer Innovation Centers where new ideas can be developed and tested. Other alternative vehicles in the United States include the following:

- *Maker/Hackerspaces:* These are essentially locations to utilize equipment that might be too steep for a startup. One such place in the United States is the Sudo Room, which may be found at: **https://sudoroom.org**.

- *Meetup Platforms:* Also known as "hackathons," these events cut to the chase and force people together to build something at lightning speed—usually in the tech industry. One such speed dating meetup organization is Startup Weekend; events may be found on their website at: **https://startupweekend.org**.

- *University Accelerators:* It's no secret that the newest generations of entrepreneurs are getting younger each day. Increasing numbers of university students are looking to start businesses right after their graduations—if not while still enrolled. Although brilliant ideas and university support are major plusses, university accelerators often don't have the resources of regular business accelerators. Check out the website for the accelerator at Stanford University: **https://startx.com**.

- *Startup Residences:* These city-funded projects support initiatives that help improve their respective communities, often combatting civic challenges. A network of startup residences known as STIR (Startup in Residence), which began several years ago in San Francisco, may be found here: **https://startupinresidence.org**.

The decision on whether it is more viable to work with an incubator, accelerator, or some other innovative support mechanism for a QOZ business depends on the stage of the entity itself. If it's a brand new concept, then you can look into an incubator-type option; if it's more developed and you are anxious to pick up the pace, then an accelerator-type option may be the right path.

Let's suppose you are "shopping" for prospective businesses in a QOZ. You've heard about QOZ legislation and want to help communities and benefit from the capital gains savings. However, you are uncertain about where to create the fund and which is the right business to start or improve. You are now like a perspective parent looking to "adopt" a business, so you ask the question: Do you want a newborn (i.e., an incubator baby business) or a (hopefully well-behaved) toddler (i.e., an accelerator)?

Once you have made your choice and moved forward, congratulations—you are the proud parent of a spanking new QOF!

CHAPTER NINE

CLARIFYING STRATEGY THROUGH MERGERS, ACQUISITIONS, AND DIVESTITURES

I'm not going to presume that every reader is fully versed on the distinctions between mergers and acquisitions (otherwise fondly known as M&A). Although the areas overlap—with one being part of the other—it would be incorrect to use them interchangeably. If the following explanations are too remedial for you, feel free to skim over the following five paragraphs and head straight to the next section heading.

A *merger* is when one company is bought by another and then folded into that organization or into one of its subsidiaries to form a unified legal entity. It's entirely possible for the reverse to occur; the company being purchased becomes the primary legal entity and the acquirer and its subsidiaries are melded into it.

There are many strategic reasons why the latter may occur, depending on the circumstance. For example, the company being purchased may have some beneficial tax advantages in its location the others do not. Or, perhaps its infrastructure is more conducive to becoming the legal centerpiece of the merger. There are also instances in which the company being purchased is actually the "bigger fish" or has a more established name brand in certain markets the acquirer seeks to enter.

An *acquisition*, on the other hand, is any time one company purchases another—whether it is merged with the acquiring company or not. A company may be bought outright in full or in part. Sometimes just a company's assets are acquired or the shareholders sell off their shares to a separate entity.

Here's another ball to throw up in the air with the M&A juggling act: *divestitures*. By the root word *divest*—i.e., ridding oneself of something that is deemed useless—you get a negative sense that the business is "no longer wanted." Sometimes the "disposal" is a strategic decision and not necessarily a sign that this part of the business is floundering in revenue or profit. For example, the parent company may feel the divestiture no longer fits the company's future direction and caters to its intended markets, which makes it something of a distraction or unnecessary burden for the organization. Meanwhile, another company may see all kinds of bright potential for the orphan and deem it as a useful strategic fit. Whatever the case, a divestiture can take the form of a piece or sections of a company that are separated from the whole and bought by another entity.

How about a fourth ball to juggle: a *spinoff.* In this instance, a divested part of a company becomes a brand new separate company that is not assimilated into the corporate hierarchy of the parent company. This could turn into an even more exciting opportunity if the spinoff is launched as an IPO.

It is important to recognize that, while a QOF can most certainly start a business, it is not able to acquire equity of an existing business. According to Tax Group Partners, "It cannot acquire interests in a partnership but can form a new partnership to acquire the assets of the partnership. Similarly, it cannot acquire stock but can form a new corporation to acquire the assets of a corporation."

The Ultimate Question: Why Do M&A?

Approximately 20,000 mergers and acquisitions take place in the United States each year, totaling in the neighborhood of $1.37 trillion dollars. Before you start taking out the pots and pans to bake something wonderful with all of that anticipated dough, it is important to recognize the fact that 70%-90% of all mergers and acquisitions fail. Forgive me for yet another metaphor, but that's a lot of goldfish to go belly up in the tank.

So, why take a risk on a merger and acquisition when, statistically speaking, it seems like a fool's errand? Furthermore, why endanger yourself—and potentially a QOZB in the process—while heading down this treacherous road?

I have several simple answers for both of these critical questions. First and foremost, let's presume that the QOZBs in question are *already struggling.* There is a strong probability that, without some form of outside assistance, they will continue to decline. Your investment in a QOF that acquires the company or merges it with another grants it an opportunity for a whole new life that would not otherwise occur. As you will discover as this chapter progresses with my Circle of Success® (COS) program, the risk of failure becomes mitigated by a clear path and commitment to ensuring the acquired company becomes a success.

Think of it like adopting a dog at a shelter. Maybe the animal looks sad and in poor health in the cage due to neglect, mistreatment, or just plain bad luck. You bring it to the veterinarian, who gives it necessary medications and treatment. Your next stop is on to the groomer to improve the dog's coat. Then you head to the pet store where you buy nutritional food and fun toys. When you bring the animal home, your spouse and children immediately fall in love with him and give him all kinds of unconditional TLC. Within just a few short weeks, you know what happens...the dog is now a beloved family member and, lo and behold, he's no longer that sad, sickly creature you first saw in the cage, but a happy, healthy, well-adjusted, playful pooch.

In the right welcoming hands, an acquired company can be a wonderful asset and family member and flourish in your hands. All too often, however, the acquisition is unjustly treated like a burden by the new entity instead of a grand business opportunity. Or, it's mistakenly viewed as a quick turnaround: gut it, stick some Band-Aids on it, dress it up, and then flip it. This is obviously far removed from the intent of QOZ legislation.

Handle M&A With Care

A QOZB acquired by the QOF should not be treated like a patient in an emergency clinic—bandaged and sent home with a prescription for pain medication. Instead, it should be viewed as a long-term, mutually beneficial relationship. I apologize in advance for trudging the dog metaphor back up again, but the message bears repeat emphasis: You wouldn't give away that beloved family member after having invested so much in its health and welfare, would you?

The upshot is this: M&As can indeed be successful, and they are an excellent path for QOFs. M&A deals fail 70%-90% of the time due to one or more of the following reasons, all of which are preventable or may be overcome through the right safeguards:

1. *Not enough due diligence was done.* It's perfectly fine to acquire a struggling company, as long as you have kicked the tires—and/or other parts of the vehicle—enough to be able to identify everything that needs repair. You need to realistically assess the cost to fix the business and the resources required to accomplish it. Some wheelers and dealers get so excited by "the hunt" and eager to close a deal that they miss problem-areas or gloss over them. Hand-in-hand with due diligence is ensuring that you don't overpay for an acquisition. The economics of the deal must work.

2. *Not enough patience.* Slow your wheels down, Mr. Earnhardt. While you may be anxious to cross that finish line and move on to the next deal, remember that you have tax reductions along the way at the five year (10%) and seven year (15%) marks. Acquiring a QOZB is not a quick flip, and you can't afford to assume that the company will turn around with a magical snap of your fingers. Often it requires some understanding of the big picture that may exist in the QOZ: cultural particulars, existing bureaucracies, resistance to change, mistrust, old habits/processes that no longer work, and so forth.

3. *Little or no involvement from the new owner(s).* The deal is done—and then what? Do you recruit an outside leader and let the chips fall where they may? Acquired companies in QOZs need oversight and support, at least in the beginning. You won't get the desired result if the company doesn't see and feel your presence and hear your vision directly from the source.

4. *Unrealistic expectations.* Yes, there is always going to be some pressure for the acquired company to perform. However, you must be mindful that the QOZB has likely undergone years of decline, and it may take a while for your influence and support to kick in and yield results. This means starting out with realistic expectations and mapping out incremental accomplishments. Think of it in terms of baby steps: The company must learn to crawl, stand up, and walk before it can run and then fly. Set smaller monthly and quarterly benchmarks to measure progress—and then *praise and reward* the teams for achieving these goals. You never want a scenario like Yahoo's

2013 acquisition of Tumblr. The social media platform was handed a monumental annual sales target of $100 million, which frightened off employees so much they abandoned ship. Yahoo paid a steep price for the error: a $712 million write-off for this disastrously managed acquisition.

5. *Poor integration.* M&As fail when the newly acquired company is not assimilated well into the new structure. From the onset, you need to ensure you have the right people aboard to help the effort, which may include consultants and new executive hires with the right experience. Everything needs to be carefully evaluated before making substantial changes. On the one hand, you have to act to ensure that problem areas are quickly identified and resolved. On the other, you don't want to throw the baby out with the bathwater and remove or change something that is the heart and soul of the acquired company.

6. *Failure to address cultural issues.* We have a twofold situation when it comes to M&As that are QOZBs. The first is the challenge every organization has when assimilating one company into another. There are always "cultural issues" in bridging the gaps between how the acquired business handles things vs. how the existing organization manages its business. Who reports to whom? Whose process is better? These decisions require numerous deep dives before initiating them. Then, once set in motion, you must seamlessly communicate the right message throughout the new organization about why these decisions were made and how they are going to work.

    The second situation is specific to the QOZB: Do issues exist that are specific to the acquired business because of the nature of its distress and/or location? The best bet, if you are a newcomer to this particular community or type of business, is to be transparent and admit when you have a steep learning curve. You need to listen carefully to the QOZB leadership and perhaps hire consultants and advisors who can help guide you and all merged entities through the transition.

7. *Lack of contingency plans for a worst-case scenario.* Bad things have been known to happen, and you can't be held responsible for what is beyond your control—namely, a recession. Typical-

ly, the areas impacted hardest by a recession are construction, financial services, and retail. On the opposite end of the spectrum, food and beverage, thrift stores, IT, repair services, and health care are among those areas that tend to be recession-resistant.

The above said, there is no need to be afraid of real estate, construction, or financial services and avoid them as a result. A wide range of industries is fair game for QOF investments and can be made to work. The reasoning behind this is simple: Economic climates are cyclical and you have a full decade for recession shockwaves to settle down and for you to realize the full potential of your investment.

Certainly, you should always be prepared for a worst-case scenario and be cautious about not overspending on QOZB improvements or taking unnecessary risks. Weathering storms is the "new norm" for businesses today, which means panic and fear won't get you through them. Ride them out by sticking as closely as you can to your long-term strategies and making smart business decisions. At the same time, be comforted knowing that, if the acquired company was able to live through past storms (such as the 2007 recession), the chances are good their business will make it through the next one—this time, with your guidance and confidence at the helm.

Some pretty smart businesspeople have had their share of M&A clunkers over the years. For the most part, however, these are preventable and/or can be minimized by confronting the aforementioned seven issues upfront through my Circle of Success program. (Patience: We're nearly there, I promise!)

There is, of course, an eighth pitfall to be wary of: *hubris.* Do not think for one second that you have the Midas touch and are immune to making mistakes. Even Warren Buffett—who has an extremely high batting average for success—has been known to slip on a few banana peels over the years with acquisition flops such as ConocoPhillips, U.S. Air, and Dexter Shoes. Like every great leader, he takes public ownership of his mistakes with his shareholders and also learns from them.

Proper execution of company strategies is a continuous process, especially when it comes to acquired QOZBs. They require enough funding, time, TLC, and space to grow. Most of all, they require your faith and support in their future success and need to be treated as an equal part of any newly formed entity you create.

Finding an M&A Match Made in Heaven

Many investors and entrepreneurs tend to be heavily real estate focused, which is perfectly fine—especially if that is your area of focus. In previous chapters we've discussed the numerous residential and commercial real estate opportunities that could be mined in a QOZ.

Real estate industrialists had something of a head start investing in QOZs because the initial drafts of the rules were overcomplicated and some investors chose to avoid going outside this arena. Now that these issues have been resolved and clarified, you can see that QOFs are not merely a real estate play. There are so many investment possibilities depending on your passions, areas of expertise, investment strategies, and the needs of the QOZ itself. Ideally, it's best when your wants and desires match up with the needs of the QOZB under consideration. In other words, what strengths do you have that can add genuine value to an acquired company or vice versa?

McKinsey identifies six types of successful acquisition approaches:

1. Improve performance.
2. Remove excess.
3. Increase market opportunity.
4. Acquire needed technology without having to build it.
5. Savings based on scalability (an increase of total production that reduces costs).
6. Pick winners early.

All of the above make complete sense for a QOZB. Number six, in particular, harkens back to our previous chapter when we explored incubators and accelerators. A main consideration, however, is determining which businesses will stimulate the most jobs in the QOZ, draw in the greatest population of new residents, and impact the communities in the most significant manner.

In the previous chapter, I cited the following as being among the hottest (but also enduring) investment trends: Energy, Health Care, Industrials,

Technology, and Telecommunications. If you were to acquire a business in one of these areas, which ones have the most potential to spark employment, demographics, and community improvement?

Looking into the future, is it so far-fetched to think that QOZBs might be acquired to help innovate and/or support an area like space tourism, as is being explored by Richard Branson (Virgin Galactic), Jeff Bezos (Blue Origin), and Elon Musk (SpaceX)? I don't think so, given that Virgin Galactic has already become a publicly traded company with claims to have sold hundreds of tickets aboard space ships at $250,000 a seat. What a bargain!

Circling Around Success

Now comes the moment you've been waiting for: Circle of Success® (COS), a customized program that provides investors, leaders, and managers with the tools needed to turn acquired QOZBs around. I've been using this original process to conduct due diligence, acquire/merge, and successfully improve twenty-two companies worldwide. I could devote an entire library to covering the principles of COS but, due to limited space, I'll only outline it in broad strokes and cross-reference to later chapters that explore a few topics in greater depth.

The best part of COS is that it specifically addresses how to avoid layoffs when acquiring a company—which tends to be the typical path of new owners. If you are doing M&A in a QOZ, the last thing you want is to buy a company and then gut it—which would be counter to everything we are attempting to accomplish with QOFs. Most likely, QOZBs are already pretty lean given that they have had to find ways to survive. Why slice and dice them further and risk penetrating a vital organ?

The good news, as you'll discover, is that one of the primary goals of COS is to spark *job growth* and *decrease unemployment* in QOZs—yet still build profit.

"How is it this even possible?" you ask.

I'm glad you asked! Stay tuned and you'll find out.

COS as Corporate Therapy

The words "corporate therapy" may sound a bit wishy-washy at first, but they're not. In my mind, this simply means that leaders must come to terms with who they are and how they lead. Are you, as a business leader and investor, taking into consideration the workforce and the community with every business decision you make?

As I've written and spoken about in the past, I believe leaders leave their mark on the world by fully living their purpose. In fact, several years ago I wrote a book on the subject, *What's My Purpose?*, in which I explain how to embark on a purpose journey to understand why we are here and how we can make a difference in the world. I won't tumble down a rabbit-hole and delve into purpose here, except to say that as a leader you need to develop one in order to have meaning in your life and work, which will translate outward to the benefit of the people in the organizations you acquire.

Once you have a purpose, I recommend taking the time to understand and establish COS prior to moving forward with your next M&A in a QOZ. This management system has been likened to corporate therapy because it focuses as much on the personal/emotional side of the equation as it does on professional/strategic tactics. No matter how analytical and nuts-and-bolts realistic you may be, you simply can't establish a successful M&A business without equally factoring in the emotional side. After all, *people* are what make any company successful—not just numbers.

As a case in point, in August 2019 the Business Roundtable—"an association of chief executive officers of America's leading companies working to promote a thriving U.S. economy..."—issued a public statement redefining the purpose of a corporation to promote "an economy that serves all." The statement doesn't mean we must turn our backs on shareholders—they remain hugely important—but rather, we should focus instead on creating long-term value that better serves investors, employees, communities, suppliers, and customers, *as well as shareholders.*

In other words, people and communities truly matter when it comes to corporate business decisions. Business with heart—now *that* is speaking my language! It's as if the twenty or so CEOs at the Business Roundtable were channeling the QOZ concept lodged in my brain when they crafted their message.

The goals of COS, therefore, dovetail nicely with the overall direction of the nation's corporate leadership:

• Enable organizations to fulfill their true potential.

• Convey meaning and understanding to the work.

- Develop goals and strategies for future action.

- Align resources in relation to strategic goals.

- Recruit, select, and retain the right people.

- Measure performance and take appropriate action.

- Inspire self-motivation for people to achieve their goals.

- Create a culture of excellence.

Are you ready to inspire excellence for the companies you acquire in QOZs and ensure success? Look no further.

The Eleven Stages of COS

COS is an ongoing system for ensuring success, no matter what stage you may be in the organizational process. Of course, it is especially useful in the beginning of M&A, so that everyone is starting at the same place with a clean slate. Given space limitations and the focus of this book, I won't be able to cover all aspects of COS—just the highlights. Consider this a primer on how a new QOZB added to your business portfolio can beat the aforementioned M&A odds. It doesn't matter whether you have purchased it whole, extracted it from a larger business, or merged it with other entities; COS is timeless and universal.

CIRCLE of SUCCESS®

As you can see in the accompanying graphic, the program consists of eleven stages divided into three rings: seven on the outer perimeter; three in the second; and one in the middle. Let's begin by exploring the second area, which consists of the three main foundations of any business:

1. *Vision:*
   - This is where it all starts: Everything extends from the Vision.
   - Brainstorm with the leadership team to create a statement of what the company should look like in the future.

2. *Mission:*
   - Work with your leadership team to craft a one-sentence statement defining what your organization is, why it exists, and its reason for being.

3. *Organizational Values:*
   - Collaborate with your leadership team to develop a list of things your company stands for (outside of revenue and profit) as its belief system.
   - Sync the values of the acquired company with the original business.

Then we proceed to the outer part of the circle:

4. *Personal Growth:*
   - Self-reflection time!
   - Establish a growth/development plan for each leader.

5. *Communications:*
   - Improve methods of company communications:
     - Determine the right frequency of messaging.
     - Assess the best formats: company meetings, team meetings, video, newsletters, and emails.
   - Involve staff in suggesting and implementing improvements.

6. *Planning:*
   - Establish a business plan.

   - Create long- and short-term goals to meet the business plan based on reasonable revenue and profit targets.

   - Make adjustments as necessary to stay on track.

7. *Organization:*
   - Create and/or improve the organizational structure to meet the business plan. (See Chapter Eleven, "Managing Management, Under-Managing the Business, and Controlling Workflow," for guidance on how to improve the inner workings of a QOZB with business mapping and other tools.)

   - Define roles and responsibilities.

   - Delegate projects and responsibilities:

     - Assign the right person for the right task.

     - Provide guidance without micromanaging.

     - Hold people accountable.

     - Acknowledge success.

8. *Staffing:*
   - Align staffing with the business plan.

   - Hire the best people.

   - Get the wrong people off the bus.

9. *Controlling:*
   - Create measurements to ensure proper execution of the business plan. (See Chapter Twelve, "Measuring Success," for more specific guidance in this area.)

   - Compare performance versus plan on a regular basis.

10. *Leadership:*
    - Inspire, empower, encourage, challenge, and lead by example.

- Attributes of a great leader: create a clear vision; recognize potential in others; develop trust; encourage excellence; demonstrate integrity; show empathy; have a sense of humor (that is workplace appropriate, of course); maintain humility; display passion for the company vision and mission (which comes a bit later); exude confidence and courage; and manage the business with a unique style.

- A great leader assumes these responsibilities: create and communicate the vision; see the big picture; recognize and assume risk; discover strengths in others and encourage their growth; and set the example for organizational values.

- Start with 360-degree feedback of leaders with professional surveys of participants, partners, supervising managers, peers, and direct reports.

- Identify major common themes: strengths and weaknesses.

- Investigate and problem-solve variations of the plan.

Last, but certainly not least, the all-important center:

11. *Results:*
    - Communicate the Vision, Mission, and Organizational Values, to the entire organization.

    - Analyze shortfalls and celebrate victories.

I cannot over-emphasize the importance of fully investing in the QOZB once acquired. This means managing—but not micromanaging—the business with heart, soul, and mind. I admit it takes some time and commitment upfront but, once you have created the COS Vision, Mission, and Organizational Values and have established a self-managing leadership team, you can gradually loosen your grip on the reigns and trust people will do their jobs and produce results.

Oh yes, there is one more thing: I haven't forgotten the all-important Board of Directors. They are so vital to the success of the QOZB that I've devoted all of Chapter Ten to this group of important people.

CHAPTER TEN

ESTABLISHING THE BOARD AS THE BOSS

In several respects, a QOZB is a business like any other organization: There are chief executives, business leaders, managers, and employees in all departments who perform roles that are vital appropriate to that particular industry. In the last chapter, we went through the organizational and leadership strategies that should be implemented when the QOZB is acquired or created.

In addition, I wholeheartedly recommend that a QOZB install a Board of Directors to help guide and continuously steer the company in the right direction.

Why is a Board so important? Having a Board can speak volumes to potential investors. First, it signals that the company is "serious" and cares deeply about its future. If the Board consists of high profile, successful professionals, that makes the company even more prestigious and attractive. Credentialed members wave a flag indicating that the company's best interests are being safeguarded and supported at all times, serving and protecting the interests of investors, shareholders, employees, and other stakeholders—including the community at large.

I'll also just blurt out one outright fact: Owners of private companies—especially sole proprietorships—are often accustomed to making all of the business decisions themselves and believe they know what's best in every situation. There are those entrepreneurs (you know who you are!) who like to control things and micromanage. This may have worked when the business was just a fledgling, but I'll tell you straight up that this will not fly—especially for a QOZB. No one person can take a QOZB to the next level on his or her own. If he or she does, it's a sign of an inflated ego, which will be detrimental to the future of the business.

A formal Board of Directors elected by the shareholders keeps everything in check (except in the form of a CEO-run Board, which you'll find out about later in this chapter). On a continuing basis, the Board votes on matters specified in its bylaws that are essential for protecting the interests of the shareholders. Later on in this chapter, we will explore other types of Boards—such as Advisory Boards—which are intended more as "expert counsel" than a decision-making entity.

All in the Family

There is a justified counter-argument against one certain type of Board, and I've experienced this several times firsthand. Answer this one question to figure out what that issue might be.

Question: What do you suppose frequently happens when a family-owned company appoints Board members?
Choose *a, b, c, d,* or *e* below:
  a) The leadership undergoes a thorough candidate search process and recruits the best, most qualified people for each Board position.
  b) The family searches Indeed.com and reviews candidates' qualifications on the site.
  c) The family places ads in the Help Wanted section of the local newspaper.
  d) The head family member asks his golfing buddies to serve.
  e) The family places every family member in a Board slot: Hubert, the owner's brother, whose last job was placing bubble gum machines in malls; Matilda, the owner's sister, who suffers from chronic narcolepsy and nods off every ten minutes; Uncle Ernie, who has a criminal record and owns an Internet gaming company; and Aunt Bessie, who knits cute outfits for her cats during Board meetings.

If you answered *e*, you would be correct! When family-owned companies install their own people in crucial Board positions, the situation more often than not becomes a hornet's nest of quirkiness, infighting, distraction, conflicts of interest, and family intrigue. The owner may be "stacking the deck" when filling Board positions so decisions always come out in her favor—which is not necessarily the best thing for the company. Or, she believes that she is doing the right thing by inserting family members in those director positions because that's what you are "supposed" to do out of love, loyalty, respect, and/or dedication to bloodlines. She may be further convinced that only family members will reciprocate her good faith choices and do what is necessary to protect the family's interests. Well, we all know how family loyalty turned out in the *Godfather* films.

You must take a hard look within yourself and answer these questions with utmost honesty:

- Are these individuals truly the best people to serve as trusted Board members?

- Do they have important wisdom to share that will improve the business?

- Do they have hidden agendas and conflicts of interest that may be detrimental to the business?

- Do they even agree on which restaurant to choose for a family dinner?

These are challenging questions for an owner to answer (especially the last one!). At the end of the day, however, the business must be given its best chance to survive and thrive. Family members tend to lack the experience, outside perspective, and objectivity necessary to provide genuinely helpful, positive, and forward-thinking contributions to the business. Sometimes they would rather make decisions that support their own hidden agendas, which may be harmful and counter to the business. One grudge from a family member can destroy a Board—and a QOZB—before it's even been born. These situations can be brutal, especially if it's a situation in which the family constitutes half the Board and wishes to overrule the other half on every issue as a power play.

If you are in the process of establishing a Board for a QOZB, I urge you to exercise caution when considering family members. Those individuals must be qualified, experienced, objective, and trustworthy, or else the business isn't going to flourish. I understand that, while it may be difficult to turn down and potentially insult a family member, you must balance that against bringing in a Board member who may stir the pot, make poor decisions, and waste your precious time having to sort out all of the bickering and misdirection.

If you happen to be an investor evaluating a QOZB family-owned business, you would be well served to take a close look at each Board member and determine if the individual is worth his or her salt. A Board consisting primarily of family members should set off flashing red lights. In *The Godfather*, Don Corleone famously said, "A man who doesn't spend time with his family can never be a real man." I agree wholeheartedly with that. But you wouldn't want Sonny (Vito's hotheaded son) or Fredo (Vito's feckless, ultimately traitorous son) on your Board, would you?

If you are the business owner recruiting Board members, never select more than one or two family members at most and, even then, be wary. If you have several family members—particularly the aforementioned Hubert, Matilda, Ernie, and Bessie—who are all seeking Board assignments, politely turn them down. You may risk insulting them in the short-term, but it's far better than the long-term damage their appointments would inflict on the business, which would likely result in family feuds anyway.

Instead, choose the *best people* who don't have conflicts of interest, yet do have strong emotional intelligence to go along with business savvy. If you happen to make the decision to install a family member, make it 100% clear that he or she understands the ground rules, obeys the charter, and respects the company Vision at all times.

Who Is Aboard the Board?

Control over the composition of the Board of Directors rests with the shareholders, who have the power to appoint a director. The shareholders can also fix the minimum and maximum number of directors. Although the Board can usually appoint a director to his or her office as well, a Board member may only be dismissed from office by a majority vote of the shareholders—provided that a special procedure is followed. The procedure is complex, and legal advice is always required.

The Board of Directors nominates its officers, which at minimum include the following people:

- **Chairman of the Board:** No, I'm not referring to Frank Sinatra. Rather, this is the individual who has the most authority on the

Board and provides leadership and direction. Sometimes known as "President," he or she ensures that the organization is acting in the best interests of its shareholders. Many Boards favor the word "Chair" to be gender neutral or specifically use "Chairwoman" or "Chairperson" if the Board leader happens to be female. The Chair is often seen as the spokesperson for the Board and the company. Additional responsibilities include:

- Providing the deciding vote in the event of a tie among Board members.

- Determining Board composition and organization.

- Clarifying Board and management responsibilities.

- Planning and managing Board and committee meetings.

- Ensuring the effectiveness of the Board.

- **Vice President:** Consider this role to be somewhat like the governmental role of Vice President of the United States. Also known as "Vice Chair," this individual serves in the absence of the President.

- **Secretary:** Though this term has become passé (and offensive to some) when referring to supportive administrative assistant roles, it's actually quite a respected Board position. The Board Secretary sends out meeting notices, prepares meeting agendas, and offers guidance on proper meeting procedures. He or she typically takes minutes at Board meetings and maintains all records. The Secretary is often the third in line to fill in if the Chair or Vice President is unavailable. In smaller organizations, the Secretary and Treasurer may be one and the same person.

- **Treasurer:** This individual is the lead financial officer, which entails a sizable responsibility. If the organization has a special finance committee, the Treasurer serves as Chair of it. Essentially, the Treasurer applies his or her finance and accounting expertise to the big picture of the business. Assuming the company has an internal CFO, the Treasurer will review the materials created by that individual, including: the budget, financial reports, tax forms, and annual audits. The Treasurer will then summarize and interpret financials for the Board's input and approval.

What Does a Board Actually Do?

Essentially, the Board of Directors hires the CEO (aka General Manager) of the business and assesses the overall direction and strategy of the business. In turn, under advisement of the Board, this individual is responsible for filling the other leadership positions and overseeing the day-to-day operation of the business.

The Board's broad purpose is to ensure the company's prosperity by collectively directing the company's affairs while meeting the appropriate interests of its shareholders and stakeholders. In addition to business and financial issues, Boards must deal with challenges and issues relating to corporate governance, social responsibility, and ethics.

Specifically, these are six of the most important functions of the Board:

1. **Recruit, supervise, retain, evaluate, and compensate the CEO/Managing Director:** Value-added Boards must aggressively search for the best possible candidate for this position. We've already emphasized the potential pitfalls of hiring a family member. Another major error I've seen is under-compensating the CEO. Managerial compensation can provide a good financial payoff in terms of attracting a top candidate who will remain committed to the role for some time.
2. **Provide big picture direction for the organization:** The Board has a strategic function in providing the Vision, Mission, and Values of the organization. These are often determined in combination with the CEO of the business. If the Vision, Mission, and Values have already been created by the leadership team, the Board should vet these materials and offer their constructive feedback and insights.
3. **Establish a policy-based governance system:** The Board must develop a series of policies for itself, Articles of Governance, which outline the rules for the group. In a sense, it's no different than a club. The policies should be broad and not so rigidly defined that they prohibit the Board from deci-

sion-making and moving the business forward. A bit later in this chapter we will cover the four types of Board governance models.

4. **Govern the organization and the relationship with the CEO:** Another responsibility of the Board is to develop a separate governance system for outlining how the entity should interact with the CEO. This would include the frequency of interaction. At the least, this includes Board of Director meetings. In between these sessions, it would also include regular check-in phone and videoconference meetings.

5. **Fiduciary duty to protect the organization's assets and members' investment:** The Board has a fiduciary responsibility to represent and protect the investor's interests in the company. This means the Board must ensure the assets of the company are kept in good order. This includes the company's human capital (employees), plant, equipment, and facilities.

6. **Monitor and control function:** The Board is in charge of the auditing process and hires the auditor. This must be done in a timely, professional manner.

Other Roles Assumed by the Board

As if all of the above isn't enough, the Board may also perform a whole bunch of other ongoing functions:

- Vet whether the company's goals and strategies are continuously in sync with the Vision and Mission.

- Create/revise/update company policies.

- Ensure that the company's organizational structure and capabilities are appropriate for implementing approved strategies.

- Develop a **PEST** analysis to assess the impact of outside forces on your business:

  - **P**olitical: political factors, such as regulations, that might impact the business.

PEST ANALYSIS

Political Factors:

Economic Factors:

Opportunities: | Threats:

Opportunities: | Threats:

YOU

Socio-Cultural Factors:

Technological Factors:

Opportunities: | Threats:

Opportunities: | Threats:

- **E**conomic: economic factors, such as unemployment rate and hints of recession, which might impact the business.

- **S**ocial: Social factors, such as baby boomers working later in life, which might impact the customer base of the business.

- **T**echnology: Technological factors, such as the shelf life of a product innovation, that might impact the business.

- Develop a **SWOT** analysis *(see chart on following page)* to assess the **S**trengths, **W**eaknesses, **O**pportunities, and **T**hreats of a business.

The Board should never be looking to execute day-to-day functions that serve the previously mentioned tasks. Instead, its role is to *delegate* the following types of things to management (which may, in turn, delegate to others in the organization):

- The directive to "make it so" when it comes to running the business and successfully implementing strategies, policies, and tasks.

- Creation of the monitoring criteria to be used by the Board.

- Safeguards to ensure that business controls are effective.

- Communication with leaders and staff within the business, as appropriate.

Another vital aspect of a Board is exercising accountability to shareholders and being responsible to relevant stakeholders on important issues, such as the following:

- Communicate to and from shareholders and relevant stakeholders.

- Understand and take into account the interests of shareholders and relevant stakeholders.

- Monitor relations with shareholders and relevant stakeholders by gathering and evaluating appropriate information.

SWOT ANALYSIS

Strengths:	Weaknesses:
Opportunities:	Threats:

- Promote the goodwill and support of shareholders and relevant stakeholders.

Governance Models

In a utopian Board, everyone gets along well, treats each other with respect, and makes smart, efficient decisions. As we know, however, great minds don't always think alike—especially when individuals have different experience, expertise, and backgrounds—and disagreements have been known to occur. Some of this is healthy in order to create solid debate and ultimately arrive at the best decision for the organization. On other occasions, well… you do your best and hope it ends amicably without injury (to egos, I mean) and effective compromise.

Since such disparities do exist, various governance models have been created to help Boards function as smoothly as possible. Examining and choosing the right model is important because it will impact the success of the value-added business.

Here are the four types of governance options:

- **CEO/General Manager focus:** In this model, the CEO dominates the Board. We can all think of situations where we have had one individual ruling a group. The Board functions as an Advisory Board and reacts to the views of the CEO, generally rubber-stamping his or her decisions. This model often emerges when you have a charismatic CEO proactively running the organization. In some cases, this is not a good model for a value-added business because the CEO isn't required or even incentivized to follow the Board's advice. This means he or she could be missing significant opportunities or making idiosyncratic decisions that will negatively impact the business—yet doesn't really care. In these instances, the Board is something of window-dressing to add prestige to the company, but without enough influence to make a substantial positive difference.

  On the opposite end of the spectrum, there are circumstances in which the CEO is recruited specifically to turn the business around—*including the Board.* I have faced such challenging circumstances on several occasions as CEO of companies that likely would have faced bankruptcy if they had continued the way they were headed. Their Boards were in shambles, past management made disastrous decisions, and most of the shareholders didn't have a clue.

  My first days with each of these companies were like repeat trips to the gates of purgatory and back. But I did exactly what had to be done and made radical changes—from playing hardball with Board members to reorganizing the companies themselves.

  One business in particular has reaped the rewards of all the tumultuous change I initiated. The company has doubled in revenue with skyrocketing EBITDA.

I'm not repeating this tale to tout my abilities, but rather, to emphasize the point that the right CEO at the right time in this model can make a tremendous difference to a company—not just to shareholders and the Board, but also to the employees, their families, the key stakeholders (vendors and customers), and the community as a whole. It takes vision, courage, and determination in order for all of this to come to fruition. It is all about trust, execution, and accountability.

- **Proactive Board:** In this model, the Board speaks as one voice. Typically, this Board is represented by the CEO of the organization, who speaks on behalf of everyone. This is a good model because it means the CEO and the Board are on the same page. It is particularly strong for entrepreneurial businesses actively pursuing emerging opportunities.

- **Geographic representation:** With this model, a Board member feels that he or she has been elected to represent individuals in a geographic location or special interest group. To better understand this model, think of an individual running for a political office and then representing the interests of the individuals located in that specific area. This is often found in large Boards consisting of twenty-four to fifty individuals. With a large group like this, there is a temptation for the directors to represent the interests of the members and investors in their geographic areas or special interest groups, rather than what might be in the best interests of the overall company. This is not a model that works well for most value-added businesses.

- **Community representation:** In this situation, the Board member is representing the community rather than the organization. An example of this is a school board, where an individual is elected to represent certain interests within the community.

If a Board member has previously served on a different Board, she may only be aware of that one specific governance model. For this reason, it is a good practice for Boards to actively investigate and discuss the models presented above and choose the right one for their respective situations.

In the case of QOZBs, the most effective Board governance model would be number two, the Proactive Board. In this instance, all directors are active and present a single voice of what is best for the organization. Since there is the bigger picture of the QOZ at stake, what works best for the organization will likely also be good for the various members, investors, and the community as a whole.

In Board We Trust

The word "trust" appears earlier in this chapter. This is an implicit part of a Board member's role. He or she is entrusted with confidential corporate documents that must remain so forever. A Board member is also trusted to provide expert counsel to the best of his or her ability. Last, but certainly not least, a Board member is trusted to look after the affairs of the company and not abuse his or her position in order to personally profit at the expense of the company, which in turn would negatively impact the shareholders, leaders, employees, and the community.

Consequently, the law imposes a number of duties, burdens, and responsibilities upon Board directors to prevent any such shenanigans. Company laws may be seen as a balance between allowing directors to manage the business and increase its profit while simultaneously preventing abuse of authority and privilege.

These are a few of the main laws Board members must abide by:

- **Malfeasance:** Proper books (financials) must be kept.

- **Debt repayment:** If a Board member attempts to "trade out of difficulty" (i.e., wrongful trading), he or she may be liable for debt and perhaps even lawsuit claims.

- **Improper purpose:** A director can only exercise his or her powers for a "proper purpose"—that is, within the limitations of what has been approved by shareholders.

- **Best interests:** A Board member must always honestly believe he or she is acting in good faith to serve the company. In the event of a conflict of interest (such as financial) between the company's interests and her own, a director must always favor the company.

- **Due skill and care:** It is assumed that the Board member will be working to his or her fullest capacity for the benefit of the company.

If problems arise, it's usually because the guidelines are not being followed. As previously mentioned, conflict occurs when the Board members meddle in the day-to-day operation of the business. Conversely, things go off the rails when the CEO heads in a direction counter to the Board's agreed upon policy decisions.

Only the Shadow Knows

In many circumstances, the law applies not only to a director, but also to a "shadow director." The person or entity nominated to, claiming, or assigned to this role provides directions or instructions to Board members, which must be followed. Under this definition, it is possible that a director or the whole Board of a holding company—as well as the holding company itself—could be treated as a shadow director of a subsidiary.

Professional advisors providing advice in their professional capacity are specifically excluded from the definition of a shadow director in the company's legislation.

How Do Board Meetings Work?

The Board, which is directly accountable to the shareholders, must meet periodically in order for the directors to discharge their responsibilities. Typically, that is accomplished with a monthly Board meeting, although some groups have reduced the number of meetings to eight or even quarterly. During these sessions, the Board members discuss and review the company's overall situation, strategy, and policies, and inform each other of progress in their individual areas of purview (which we will cover soon).

Each year, the company should hold an annual general meeting (AGM) at which the directors must provide a report to shareholders on the performance of the company and future plans and strategies. At this juncture, they also submit themselves for re-election to the Board.

A director—or the Secretary at the request of a director—may call a Board meeting. Each director must be given reasonable notice of the meeting, stating its date, time, and place. Seven days are commonly provided, but business circumstances and individual schedules may shorten or lengthen this time frame.

Every meeting must have a Chair, whose duties include creating the agenda, ensuring that the proceedings are properly conducted, and focusing the Board discussion on the intended subject matter. Everyone is entitled to express his or her views during the meeting. The decisions made during the proceedings must adequately reflect the views of the meeting as a whole. More often than not, the Chair is required to sign off on the minutes of the meeting to be certain everything has been correctly documented.

If a Chair is not present within five minutes of the start time fixed for the meeting or is unwilling to preside, those directors in attendance may elect one of their members as Chair of the meeting.

Some Advice on Advisory Boards

If for some reason you are unable to establish a formal Board of Directors like what has been described throughout this chapter, I strongly encourage that you create an Advisory Board for the QOZB. This is less formal than a traditional Board, but many of the precepts mentioned earlier may still apply. The benefits are that there would be resources available to provide expert consultation on major business decisions, regular recordkeeping, and focused attention on the company's Vision, Mission, and Values. A strong list of credentialed Advisory Board members still has the potential to make a company as appealing to investors as a formal Board of Directors.

There are many ways to create an effective Advisory Board, and its structure may depend on the industry and the size of the business. This is especially important to install for a sole proprietorship; the owner's heart may be in the right place, but he or she can't be expected to be an expert at everything.

The QOZB may elect to hire an outside firm to serve in an advisory capacity. The consulting company might bring in various experts as needed based on the company's circumstances. In other cases, this firm may offer peer-to-peer counsel to the CEO or owner on a regular basis.

Ideally, an Advisory Board would include established leaders from the QOZ community itself to ensure that every effort is being made by the company to do what is best for both the business and the area.

Another route is for the leadership to create what is known as a "mastermind" group. Originally conceived by Napoleon Hill (perhaps best known for the classic book *Think and Grow Rich*), a mastermind is an assemblage of top industrialists, business owners, and entrepreneurs who meet the owner on a semi-recurring basis—often over a dinner—to brainstorm, share ideas, offer networking contacts, and problem-solve. If you are a business owner with a QOZB who is resistant to having a Board of any kind, this is an excellent way to pick the brains of genuine authorities without the pressure of a Board.

Boards with Purpose

In the last chapter, I introduced the statement from the August 2019 Business Roundtable and how CEOs are now looking to create organizations that better serve investors, employees, communities, suppliers, and customers, *as well as shareholders.*

I believe that, by extension, Boards should follow this same ideology and factor *purpose* into their deliberations.

In a Directors & Boards Forum called "Character of the Corporation," Delaware Supreme Court Chief Justice Leo Strine discussed the larger role Boards can play ensuring the community is taken into account with major business decisions. In attempts to please shareholders and/or boost profit, some Boards in the past may have been inclined to counter a company's environmental, social, and governance (ESG) initiatives. I can only imagine how disheartened the company leadership and employees felt when their noble efforts were derailed by the Board.

My thinking is right along those lines with the wave of logic spurred on by the Business Roundtable Statement. Boards should strive to encourage business leadership and staff to work toward the "greater good," especially in the case of QOZBs.

Now that we've established how a QOZB should be created with Board oversight and input, we are ready to proceed to reaching the next level of successful QOF profitability: *managing management,* aka the company leadership itself.

CHAPTER ELEVEN

MANAGING MANAGEMENT, UNDER-MANAGING THE BUSINESS, AND CONTROLLING WORKFLOW

If you are following the Circle of Success® as described in Chapter Nine and have an established Board of Directors (or Advisory Board) and the ideal CEO (perhaps yourself) in place as laid out in Chapter Ten, you are already more than halfway toward turning a QOZB into a functioning business with a bright future capable of achieving success.

But how do you know what is the right amount of involvement from management? Do you blaze through everyone and right the ship all by yourself—or entrust the leadership team to take care of business all on its own? How do you determine when you are *managing* versus *micromanaging*?

Truth be told, there isn't a definitive answer. Every organization and type of business requires a different approach—and one size doesn't fit all. One thing I can tell you: When companies fail, it's because leadership ends up falling into one extreme camp or the other. Either the business fumbles along without enough direction, or it heads the opposite route and becomes over-managed to the point of second-guessing and frustrating the leadership team, which causes confusion and a mass employee exodus. In the latter instance, employees can't have multiple people directing—especially if they end up contradicting each other.

The ideal situation is to have balance. Once the team and business foundations are all in place, the fledgling QOZB should be able to reach a cruising altitude and soar straight towards its intended destination. At this point, it is hoped that having regularly scheduled check-ins and reviews with the leadership team will serve as a GPS and ensure everything is humming along on course. During the check-ins, the Board and the CEO would provide guidance, support, experience, and resources as necessary in case something seems to be going awry or if a storm is advancing toward the company.

As the company proves itself to be competent, transparent, and trustworthy, the reins must gradually be loosened. You are like a proud papa (or mama) watching his (or her) little girl ride a bike independently for the first time with the training wheels removed. After that, while letting go, you are supervising to verify that she is always wearing a helmet, following the rules of the road, and letting you know where she is going and what time she will be home.

Now...we know for a fact that not all children follow their parent's instructions. Similarly, companies have been known to steer off the road, receive speeding tickets, get into traffic accidents, and get lost with a flat tire, no spare, and no cell phone signal.

The following are a few warning signs you need to watch for and protect against: expenses and costs getting out of hand; revenue continuously dipping lower each month; employee engagement sinking while turnover is rising; products releasing late and/or with faulty components; customer complaints mounting up; and so forth.

How you respond to these things as they occur can either serve to plug the holes in the ship or plunge it right to the bottom of the ocean. The trick is in knowing when you should give the organization a slap-on-the-wrist warning, a parking ticket, or something far more severe (such as termination).

If any of the above issues are causing rumblings in the organization and you are losing sleep as a result, this is the first question to ask: *Are you 100% certain that the company is as streamlined, automated, and efficient as it can possibly be?* Do bottlenecks exist, yet you can't easily identify their *root causes* (i.e., sources) in order to fix the problems?

If the answer is *Yes*, you must resist your impulse to swoop right in like a superhero and try to solve everything all at once *for* the team instead of *with* the team. The risk here is that leaders and team members will think you are a know-it-all micromanager and will develop resentments toward you. Feeling defensive, they might be change-resistant and protective about their current systems and processes—sometimes to the point of attempting to conceal or hide certain things they feel are fine just as they are.

So, what is my recommended solution to improve the inner workings of a QOZB? Dive right back in to COS, the Circle of Success, which

I introduced in Chapter Nine. Stage 5 begins with business mapping techniques that offer tools on how to identify the issues needing to be addressed in your organization. This Stage next explores process improvement methods to help create an organizational workflow that is smooth, efficient, self-corrects, and has a decreasing amount of mistakes in its processes and systems.

Mapping the Future

Business maps visually depict the system of relationships and processes within and around organizations. Used effectively, they generate a common understanding of these processes and relationships. Business maps also provide a framework for discussions memorializing how an organization currently works, identifying areas that must be improved in order to run the business more efficiently and create visions for the future.

Why are these maps and the revelations derived from them so vital to a QOZB? The business landscape is changing so rapidly at every level—and not just in terms of technology—that the business must be nimble and flexible enough to adapt to anything that may come its way.

Adaptability means being equipped to rapidly change processes to meet new environmental variables, which may include innovation and challenges. In order for organizations to be adaptable, the people working within them must have a deep understanding of how their organization works as a system and interacts with the surrounding business environment.

These are seven specific reasons why business maps are invaluable:

1. Developing an awareness of the network of processes through which the organization's work is accomplished.
2. Creating an inventory of the organization's processes.
3. Identifying which processes are causing the organization to fall short of its goals.
4. Collecting process performance data in search of improvement opportunities.
5. Defining the output necessary to facilitate suitable input to the subject process.
6. Defining the output the subject process must provide as input to other processes.

7. Helping team members understand the following: project scope, goals, inputs/outputs to/from other processes; and the relationship of their project to other process improvement projects in the organization (potential conflicts, potential synergies, etc.).

The Types of Business Maps

Although there are many variations of business maps, we will address three basic types that have proven particularly useful in improving organizational performance when aligned to the Circle of Success process.

Type 1: Process Relationship Maps
A Process Relationship Map *(see chart p.144)* represents a high-level view of an organization. In this case, it graphically depicts the relationship between the organization's process and how it delivers its products and/or services to customers. The Process Relationship Map shows—through inputs and outputs—how each process interacts with the others.

Type 2: Process Maps
A Process Map *(see chart p.145)* describes the way work is accomplished. It visually presents the sequential steps involved in converting a specific input into an output and offers documentation describing each step. The Process Map should be so clear that anyone studying it with the written document would be able to execute the business process. If something is unclear, you already know there is a problem with the process.

Type 3: Function Relationship Maps
A Function Relationship Map offers another high-level view of an organization. This depicts the key relationships—expressed as inputs and outputs—among the organization's internal functions (departments), customers (consumers), and suppliers (vendors).

Business Mapping Guidelines

When preparing business maps, work typically progresses from rough drafts to final clean documents. Along the way, questions typically arise regarding how or where a box or line should be positioned on the map.

PROCESS RELATIONSHIP MAP

The following Process Relationship Map represents a high-level view of an organization. It depicts the relationship between the processes as it seeks to deliver its product to customers.

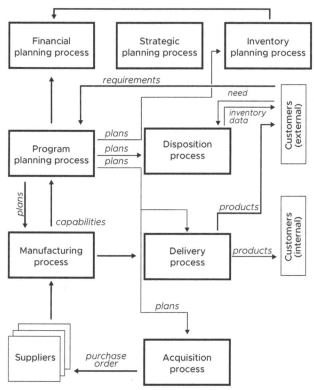

While there are no "right" answers to such questions, there are some ACE (Accuracy, Clarity, and Emphasis) objectives to help provide some guidance:

1. **Accuracy:** Is the map an accurate representation of the process/relationship?
2. **Clarity:** Is the map easy-to-understand with minimal instructions?
3. **Emphasis:** Is there a particular point or observation about this process/relationship that needs to be communicated? Does the map accomplish this?

PROCESS MAP

The following Process Map depicts the way work is accomplished. It maps out sequential steps involved in converting a specific input to a specific output.

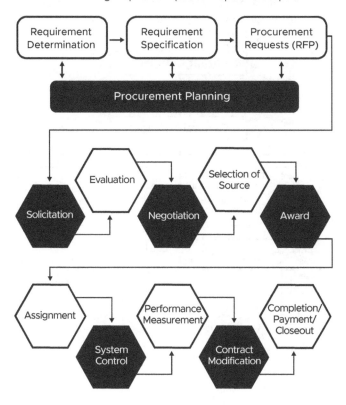

Once a QOZB has created its business maps and there is a universal understanding of how everything operates, the company is then ready to tackle the more sophisticated steps of utilizing process management systems to improve systems and workflows.

You may be asking: *How do we approach this massive task?*

Answer: Start with the number *six*.

Six Sigma Isn't a Fraternity

People often wonder whether "Six Sigma" and "Lean" are the same thing or if one is a subset of the other. That is because both are focused on

FUNCTION RELATIONSHIP MAP

The following Function Relationship Map offers a high-level view of an organization. It depicts the key relationships between the organization's internal functions (departments), and its customers and suppliers.

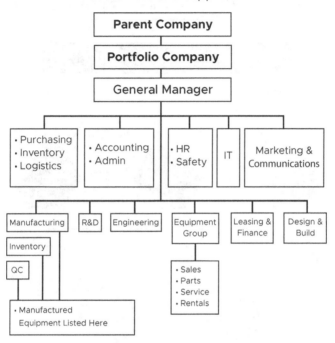

organizational improvement. Occasionally, they are used in tandem. The main difference between the two is that Lean is focused primarily on cutting costs and eliminating waste, whereas Six Sigma seeks to reduce errors. One process is not necessarily better than the other. Sometimes a company is unsure if cost, waste, errors, or a combination of all three is the main concern, so they undergo both processes to identify and resolve all issues at once.

Let's tackle Six Sigma first. The word *sigma* is a statistical term that measures how far a given process deviates from perfection. It is a way to measure quality and performance. The central idea behind Six Sigma is that, if you can pinpoint how many defects exist in a process, you can systematically figure out how to eliminate them.

These are the principles of what Six Sigma is and is not:

- It is not an add-on to normal business activities.

- It is an integrated part of the improvement process.

- It is management methodology driven by data.

- It focuses on projects that will produce measurable business results.

- It is not a standard, a certification, or a metric-like percentage (although individuals may become certified in Six Sigma, as we will address).

- *Sigma* represents a value from 1 to 6 that signifies the maximum number of defects per million:
    - 1 Sigma = 690,000 defects/million = 31% accurate
    - 2 Sigma = 308,537 defects/million = 69.1463% accurate
    - 3 Sigma = 66,807 defects/million = 93.3193% accurate
    - 4 Sigma = 6,210 defects/million = 99.3790% accurate
    - 5 Sigma = 233 defects/million = 99.9767% accurate
    - 6 Sigma = 3.4 defects/million = 99.999997% accurate

- It is about reducing variation.

- It is about proving the facts before acting.

A Six Sigma project must:

- Have financial impact or significant strategic value.

- Produce results that exceed the amount of effort required to obtain the improvement.

- Require analysis to uncover the root cause of an identified problem.

- Solve a problem that is not easily or quickly solvable using traditional methods.

- Improve performance by greater than 70% over existing performance levels.

The focus of a Six Sigma project is to solve a business problem such as:

- Ensuring the overall success of the organization.

- Reducing costs.

- Increasing customer satisfaction.

- Improving employee performance and job satisfaction.

- Maximizing process capability.

- Growing output capacity.

- Reducing cycle time.

- Lowering amount of excess inventory.

- Building greater revenue potential.

Train Your Own COS Master

So, how do you get started on such an investigative undertaking and ensure it is handled properly? The first thing to do is invest in training a talented and trusted team leader to study and master the COS process. Depending on the size and complexity of your organization, you may end up having *several* workflows investigated at the same time, which means you need one person (not you!) to oversee the entire endeavor and other COS Masters.

In addition, you may also want these same individuals to undergo Six Sigma training, which involves a certification process that results in the graduate ultimately earning a Black Belt. (Don't worry: No one actually gets harmed from this process.)

Once your COS Master (and/or Black Belt) is in place and charged with initiating the process improvement launch throughout the company, set reasonable time frames, goals, and expectations for him or her with regular check-ins to monitor progress. As previously mentioned, the main caution here is that—aside from brief review meetings with participating teams—process improvement should not be an "add-on" of time for employees or be viewed as "extra work."

In particular, the COS Master must have certain duties temporarily reassigned so that he or she can excel in this role without feeling any undue burden. The Master will already be aware from his or her training that the process for the rest of the staff should not interfere with their normal responsibilities. Everyone's time is incredibly valuable, and it would be antithetical for the initiative to do anything that might increase workflow time or cause products to go off-schedule.

A Roadmap for Implementation

A Six Sigma initiative begins with approval from the top down, followed by these five steps:

1. Formalize the overall COS initiative in the organization by establishing goals and installing infrastructure.
2. Deploy the initiative by assigning, training, and equipping the staff.
3. Implement projects and improve performance.
4. Expand the scope of the initiative to include additional organizational units.
5. Sustain the initiative through re-alignment, re-training, and evolution.

A Lean Mean Machine

Lean, in contrast to Six Sigma, in a business context refers to continuously improving towards the ideal and achieving the shortest possible cycle time through the tireless reduction of waste. This concept in America dates as far back as Benjamin Franklin, who heavily influenced the production-saving efforts of Henry Ford in his car manufacturing plant. The word *Kaizen* is a Japanese term that literally means "continuous improvement." With Kaizen, "good enough" is never enough. In other words, no process is ever perfect.

The phrase *Lean manufacturing* was coined in the 1980's and has its roots in the Toyota Production System (TPS). Three books have since shaped the ideologies of Lean: *The Machine That Changed the World* (James P. Womack, et. al.), *Lean Thinking* (also Womack, et. al.), and *The Toyota Way* (Jeffrey Liker). I've also written an ebook on the subject, *Lean Process and Six Sigma*.

These are the guiding principles of Lean:

• Elimination of waste in all processes.

• Expansion of capacity by reducing costs and shortening cycle times.

• Focus on what is important to the customer.

Here are a few examples of Lean projects:

• Reduced inventory.

• Reduced floor space.

• Quicker response times and shorter lead times.

• Decreased defects, rework, and scrap.

• Increased overall productivity.

Understandably, people tend to panic when they hear words like "reduction" and "cut costs." They believe their jobs will be at stake as a result of a Six Sigma or Lean investigation being set in motion. This couldn't be further from the case; eliminating people is not at all the objective. In fact, a residual benefit of a Six Sigma and/or Lean initiative is that it will save time, money, and resources, which generally means things will be easier and better for the people who perform the actual work. One hypothetical outcome that could result is the justification of purchasing a new cutting-edge piece of equipment that involves less physical lifting, which saves time—and employee back strain.

My approach is always to get the right person in the right job at the right time with the right training. If, however, the COS process involving Six Sigma does reveal more staff than is necessary—which usually would occur within ninety days or less from the start of the initiative—I always ask a simple question: *How did unqualified employees end up in the wrong jobs in the first place?* More often than not, it's due to: poor leadership; bad hiring practices; lack of procedures, processes, and goals (or clarity around them); and/or zero accountability.

If that is revealed to be the case, the fault lies not with the employees. It signals that there is a much bigger leadership issue here and more radical changes need to occur at the top management level than at the bottom.

The Best Laid Plans...

We all know that snafus can and will happen, no matter how exceptional the workflow and how improved the organization becomes from the COS effort. We are all humans, after all, and no one is perfect. (And, as we know, machines break down all the time...)

The main thing is to create a culture in which everything is transparent and people are comfortable enough to admit to a mistake. The best thing the company can do is thank the employee for owning it and stressing the importance of learning from it. The objective is not to assign blame; in fact, people should be *praised* for their honesty. Once the root cause is revealed, it's time to acknowledge it, forgive the individual, and move on.

There may, however, be situations in which an error or bottleneck is not self-evident. This is when you do what is known as a *post-mortem*, which sounds far ghastlier than it actually is. This is simply a process to help determine the root cause (yes, we are back to that again) of the issue and then solve it. Usually the team that is involved meets, trouble-shoots the problem, and offers proposed solutions for it without management interference (except as a check-in).

Once an organization has completed COS and is truly Lean, there should be limited need to once again undergo another Six Sigma process. If the mindset of the company is *continuous improvement*, the QOZB will already be well equipped to adapt to new demands of its customers, the never-ending advancements in technology, and the constantly evolving state of business itself.

This doesn't mean that the business is being run without "goals and controls" to ensure the ship stays on course. Various checks and balances must be established in order for the CEO, the Board of Directors (or Advisors), and the investors to remain in the loop. The fact of the matter is that it's much better for topline news about the company—good, bad, or somewhere in the middle—to be consistent, transparent, understandable, and accurate. No one at the top level can ever afford to be blindsided—and the truth always does rise to the surface at some point. It's crucial to bring information out into the open while action may still be taken before it's too late. This is precisely why Chapter Twelve, "Measuring Success," is so important for QOZBs.

MEASURING SUCCESS

What truly signifies "success" in a QOZB?

As referenced in Chapter Nine, in August 2019 the Business Roundtable declared an end to shareholder primacy in favor of *all* stakeholders: investors, employees, communities, suppliers, and customers, as well as shareholders. Companies are left with a quandary with regard to pleasing so many parties and knowing what measurements of success make sense across the board (as it were).

Overall organizational success may mean different things to different leaders, depending on the circumstances. Some companies emphasize revenue growth and market share, whereas others primarily consider EBITDA. There are also cases in which improved organizational stability, greater customer satisfaction, and/or increased employee engagement are prioritized areas of focus out of the gate.

For QOZBs, all of these are equally important. Let's also not forget there are important considerations regarding the company's employment statistics and its impact on the QOZ community itself from the QOF investment. We'll cover all of this as this chapter progresses.

Most investors are anxious to see immediate, tangible results on their investments. I wholeheartedly relate to that. Who doesn't want to see a struggling company make a miraculous financial turnaround in under a year? In the case of QOZBs, however, I recommend patience and support as the company takes baby steps toward achieving realistic goals. You have plenty of time to make money on the company and save on capital gains. The objective isn't to lower a sledgehammer if a company doesn't produce overnight results. A little TLC and encouragement can go a long way in helping earn the trust of the QOZB leadership and employees, which will ensure they are all fully committed to achieving the established goals.

That said, checks and balances must be in place to measure the progress being made toward achieving success. The leaders of your business need to know that you are paying attention and care about what is happening. You need transparency about news—whether it's good, bad, or somewhere in the middle. You most certainly didn't invest all of your time, money, and expertise for a write-off. If you set realistic expectations upfront and explain your methodology for ownership and accountability, there should never be any surprises.

The Dirty Dozen: 12 Steps for Effective Delegation of Responsibility and Authority

Of course, I'm being tongue-in-cheek with the "dirty" reference above. At first some people feel like "big brother" (or "big mama") is watching them by setting ground rules for delegation and ownership. After that initial pushback—which is largely out of fear—you will find that the business leaders appreciate being able to fully understand and anticipate what is being expected of them. It ensures that everyone stays on top of his or her goals and nothing important slips through the cracks. The worst thing is to have a project go off-course and then for everyone to shrug his or her shoulders and declare, "It wasn't my responsibility!" This is why my Twelve Steps below are so invaluable.

Step One: Select the right person for the job.
This seems pretty obvious, doesn't it? You want to assign a project to the individual who has the most suitable talents and experience. Sometimes a "stretch goal"—assigning a brand new task to a person who seems up to learning a challenge—makes sense, as long as you provide the person with appropriate training, coaching, and support along the way.

There is one important caveat here: Don't take a chance on a less experienced person if there is any doubt in your mind whether the person is capable of managing the project or not. This is especially true if the stakes are high and the success of the enterprise rests on the initiative.

Step Two: Provide all information freely and in a timely manner.
It stands to reason that someone who is assigned responsibility needs to have all of the tools necessary to get the job done. This includes a green

light to get started and receipt of all essential documents and information on the start date. I can't tell you how many times I've seen a project go south because the delegated party didn't receive something crucial; sometimes it's as simple as a stakeholder's contact information (or the authority to contact that person directly).

Step Three: Focus on results.

Some leaders assigning tasks get caught up in the minutiae and micromanage every detail. They really like to be involved, perhaps because they are so accustomed to being a *doer*—an independent worker bee, not a leader. Another way of saying this is that they redirect the employee on *how* to accomplish the task because it's not the precise way they would have done it. Here's my two cents: If the employee is showing results and not breaking any company policies, let her fly. If there are mistakes along the way, you can do a post-mortem afterward and use the takeaways as teachable moments for the next time. If, however, you constantly interrupt and criticize, the employee will flounder.

Step Four: Delegate through dialogue and follow-up.

Always, always, always talk through the project before dropping it on someone's lap. (Did I stress *always* enough?) Ask the employee to repeat back the instruction to ensure understanding. Encourage feedback and questions. Complete the communication loop by summarizing everything in a follow-up email. And, once again, encourage questions! When these questions come your way, answer them immediately. Do not let the person sit around twiddling her thumbs while the email gets buried deeper in your inbox. If you promise her a response by a certain date, be sure to deliver on it.

Step Five: Set firm deadlines.

Deadlines do matter and it is imperative that you hold people accountable to them. When due dates are established and presented, make sure the employee understands them and repeats them back. If there is pushback about being able to make a deadline at the onset, do your best to accommodate it. It's far better to move something out in the beginning than to have it run behind schedule several steps later in the process.

Step Six: Provide the necessary resources.

When a project is assigned to an employee, verify that the employee has enough people, money, and equipment to complete it on time and according to the company's quality standards. Shortchanging an employee on any of these fronts—or even delaying approvals on them—sets the project up for failure.

Step Seven: Give the entire job to one person.

Sometimes leaders mistakenly assign project management to two or more people. The theory is that it's "less of a burden" on one person to spread out the responsibility. This is another road to disaster. Why? The answer is simple: There are always disagreements and power plays that inevitably occur, which only serve to delay and derail the project, as well as cause confusion among stakeholders on the team about who is running the show. Or, if something goes awry, you have a scenario in which each project manager blames the other. (All you need to do is watch an episode of any reality TV show and you'll know what I'm talking about.) Accountability must boil down to one recognizable person at the helm.

Step Eight: Offer guidance and advice without interfering.

This is something of an extension of Step Three and bears emphasis and repeating: Do not micromanage! I heard of one specific case in which a company President assigned a task to a leader who had assumed his previous job title. The President only knew one way of getting the job done: *his way.* Try as he might, this leader could not get the job done to the President's expectations because he trashed his work every week and insisted on restarting from the beginning. When the project failed, the President placed all of the blame on the leader saying, "I told you that you should have done it my way." Well, that's *exactly why it failed!* Instead, you want to *coach* the employee and offer advice that he or she can take or leave. Never do the work *for* the employee.

Step Nine: Establish a "goal and control" system.

Just like there are goals for the overall organization, there must also be goals in place for each specific project. (See the next main heading, "Setting Business Goal Criteria," for guidance on goal setting.)

The owner of this goal would likely benefit from utilizing project management software that breaks tasks down into digestible chunks with frequent reminders of benchmark due dates. My disclaimer here is that, whatever software the organization uses, make sure it doesn't take more time to update and manage than the work involved in the actual project.

Step Ten: Support the person in any disputes that may arise.

There is nothing more frustrating for a project manager assigned a task than to have people stand in her way. This happens all too frequently in business. Coworkers may have all kinds of reasons for causing roadblocks that lead to internal feuds: unclear company priorities; lack of resources throughout the organization; creative differences; lack of respect for the other's expertise; turf wars; battles for credit; etc.

If you get wind of any such nonsense, you need to nip it in the bud right away to avoid any project delays while rallying to provide aid to your project manager. Your role is to step in and grease the wheels when necessary to gain cooperation throughout the organization. If you think it's best to let the employee "tough it out" and "learn how to deal with it," you are making a grave mistake. The dispute with the other employee will continue to fester and damage the outcome, not to mention the emotional pain and suffering your employee will endure. Sometimes a simple explanation to the other employee and his or her manager by citing the project's connection to the Vision, Mission, and overall company goals will be enough to resolve the problem.

Step Eleven: Follow-up—don't abdicate.

The opposite end of Step Eight may also cause significant problems. A project will not succeed if the leader doesn't check-in at regular intervals. Delegation, ownership, and empowerment are critical, but that doesn't mean you are entirely removed from the process. The ideal scenario is to have benchmark dates written into the project schedule to hold the team accountable: reviews, updates, and progress reports. You will want to do this 1:1 with the employee and, when appropriate, with other leaders in the organization as well.

Step Twelve: Give full credit to the person and team when they succeed and take full responsibility yourself for failure.

There is nothing better for employee morale than when a project meets with success and the people involved receive acknowledgment and praise for the accomplishment. The bosses who feel "It's the employee's job" and move on to the next task without demonstrating such appreciation will not receive the same level of support and enthusiasm the next time around. Human beings require positive reinforcement of what they have done well—even when they don't express such a need. Compensation in the form of a raise, bonus, or promotion is always welcome, but research has shown that taking the time to recognize employees is even more effective to employee job satisfaction and retention.

Unfortunately, failure sometimes does occur in an organization. People are human and mistakes get made. Often it is best for you, as the leader, to assume full responsibility for having initiated and delegated a project that didn't pan out.

There are occasions, however, when it's plain to everyone that the Project Manager didn't get something right. Rather than pointing a finger and assigning blame, establish a culture whereby the Project Manager can comfortably own up to his or her mistakes without fear of retribution or embarrassment. When this occurs, I highly recommend that the Project Manager create a post-mortem meeting and written report involving all key stakeholders to determine the root cause(s) of what went wrong and initiate specific steps to prevent these issues from being repeated in the future.

After the post-mortem is done, what do you think you should do? Praise the employee, of course, for demonstrating ownership! It takes courage to openly admit a well-intended failure. When one person is recognized for handling this professionally, others will follow suit and also realize it's safe to be transparent when things go wrong.

Setting Business Goal Criteria

Step Nine already outlined the necessity of goal setting. Now we'll dive into specifics on how to create *effective* goals and monitor their progress.

Be SMART.

For every project, I recommend establishing three-to-five topline "SMART" goals, a strategy often implemented by human resource professionals with regard to annual employee performance. The acronym stands for: *Specific, Measurable, Attainable, Relevant, and Timely.*

A one sentence example of a SMART goal would be something like this:

Increase website search engine traffic 20% by June 30 of this year. As you'll note, it's Specific (increase website traffic), Measurable (20%), Attainable (based on past history), Relevant (business revenue depends upon it), and Timely (the June 30 deadline, which adds urgency). In order to accomplish this goal, the Project Manager may need to perform a host of subset tasks, including: enlist others for assistance (i.e., experts in marketing); spend money (i.e., on search engine advertising); conduct research (i.e., focus groups or checking out competition); upgrade the website (i.e., provide direction to IT); and so forth.

Clarify alignment.

In this instance, we aren't referring to the alignment of your car. This is in terms of costs, priorities, and being in sync with the overall company goals, Vision, Mission, and strategies set in motion. Further, goals need to be aligned with revenue and profit targets. If the goals don't match up, the organization will fall out of alignment, causing loss of focus, rampant discord, and missed opportunities. When a project is misaligned in any of the aforementioned areas, it is a strong sign that the endeavor is not worth all of the effort (at least at this time).

Assess performance.

Step Eleven refers to regular check-ins and updates. Specific review dates for 1:1 and group meetings should be established in advance and placed on the calendar. These can be biweekly, monthly, bimonthly, or quarterly, depending on the size of the project and the schedule. At each meeting, the Project Manager—utilizing the Goal and Control Report (read ahead for more on this)—shares topline performance updates (again, not the *how*) and compares progress toward achieving the target goals.

If everything is on course, it becomes a time for recognition and appreciation. If things are tipping over the rails, *do not berate the Project Manager*; instead help him or her propose solutions to get things back on track. You don't need to come up with the solutions for the employee; empower him or her to develop them independently. If it turns out that the Project Manager and the team are struggling based on resources (money, time, people, or equipment) or cooperation from others, see what approvals you can provide to add more fuel to help the machine run as smoothly as possible.

The Goal and Control Checklist

As specified in Step Eleven, organizations from the top level down need to stay informed of progress on key initiatives by setting up a review meeting. This is a *check-in*—not a "bed check" for the sake of going through the motions or to "get anyone" in terms of falling behind or being off-track. It is a genuine attempt to ensure everything is running smoothly and communication is functioning as well as it should. Sometimes a misunderstanding is caused by unclear instruction from you—the leader who assigned the task. Simple pre-arranged check-ins at regularly established intervals can nip such problems in the bud and put things back on course.

Whether the check-in is being conducted by the executive team or by the actual team that is performing the work, the same rules apply. You need to have the following Goal and Control Checklist in place to ensure everything is covered in a professional and thorough manner.

1. *Everyone must show up on time.*

    Lateness is a sign of disrespect. Everyone—including the CEO—is incredibly busy, but that doesn't excuse being late. Time is too valuable to waste. I believe that it is perfectly acceptable to start the meeting without people if they are running late. If and when they show up, you should not reopen matters already discussed, as that is a further nuisance to those in attendance. I know of one President who typically showed up twenty minutes late and then insisted on trudging up matters already discussed and decided upon by subordinates. Nine of ten times he reversed the decision already made by someone else, which added insult to injury and frustrated people. Do not be that kind of leader.

    Note that "showing up on time" also means coming to the meeting prepared with prep work, documents, laptops, and anything else that may be essential for the meeting. If materials are handed out to you in advance, be sure to review them prior to the meeting.

2. *Ensure meeting consistency.*

    As mentioned, meetings should be added to everyone's calendar on a regular basis (biweekly, monthly, quarterly, or whatever is appropriate). The duration of the meeting should consistently be one-two hours. If a meeting ends up being shorter than planned, people will be thanking their maker (as well as you, specifically) for time handed back to them. However, no one appreciates when a meeting goes overtime, as it backs up schedules and causes one meeting to crash into another (and work to fall behind). When a meeting runs over, it's usually a sign that it's been poorly run and/ or someone has chewed up the time by being garrulous.

3. *Prepare and distribute the agenda one week in advance of meeting.*

Having a well-prepared agenda sent in advance is critical for the meeting to be a success. Not only does it set expectations of attendees, it offers everyone a chance to prepare ahead of time and perhaps even make a suggested change to the agenda while there is time to do so. During the meeting itself, the agenda keeps everyone focused and helps prevent the meeting from running overtime.

4. *For every meeting, the first agenda item must be a comparison of where things stand versus the goal.*

Placing the performance status first sets the tone for the entire meeting and keeps the priorities straight. If things are going according to plan, then everyone knows this will be a smooth ride. If things are off-kilter, it's best to bring that out in the open right away and spend the meeting time honing in on how to right the ship.

5. *Team members should concisely report results in comparison to plan.*

All team members must be trained on how to focus on the metrics and results in their areas that matter and move the needle. Additionally, they should be able to articulate clearly and succinctly what is happening in their departments and answer questions— no matter which executive might be in the room.

During the meeting, previous benchmark goals should also be reviewed to provide progress updates.

6. *Encourage team problem solving when goals are off-target.*

If a project is facing obstacles, a certain amount of time should be allotted on the agenda for brainstorming. If the solution doesn't present itself during this allotted meeting time frame, the team should take it offline and resolve it independently (or else it could drag on for an eternity). Their efforts would be reviewed at the next meeting.

7. *If corrective action is required, the Chair decides on next steps.*

    In every business scenario there needs to be a clear-cut decision-maker, especially when things are heading in the wrong direction. It's unlikely everyone will agree with your decision, but they will appreciate that at least one has been made and that progress can resume on the project. The worst situation is a wishy-washy leader who can't make decisions and hangs on to them forever.

8. *Negotiate goals for the next meeting and circulate the final version.*

    After a goal has been accomplished and the relevant parties have received their due praise, it's time to continue to keep the train rolling by discussing goals to be accomplished by the next meeting. It's important to memorialize these newest goals explicitly in writing and circulate them among all stakeholders.

    How soon we forget what was agreed upon! In all probability, business as we know it would implode if we relied solely on human memory. Here is my philosophy on the matter: After fourteen days, we forget 79% of what we've heard. After seven days, we forget 65% of what we've heard. After just one day, we forget 46% of what we've heard. These percentages are all the more reason to write down what was agreed upon.

9. *Move to the next item on the agenda.*

    Without missing a beat, the meeting Chair must then continue straight to the next item on the agenda. While there is a temptation to make small talk between agenda items, I recommend plowing straight on through to ensure the meeting doesn't go overtime and everything gets covered. Stick to the business at hand and keep the momentum going.

10. *Assign responsibility for action steps.*

    As with goals, any action items (or just plain follow-ups) must be assigned to specific individuals. Trust me when I say that anything open-ended or without a clear owner will remain undone.

11. *Set target dates.*

    It's equally as important to establish reasonable target dates by when the action steps will be completed. The individual assigned the responsibility has the all-important role of speaking up if the date is unreasonable based on her schedule and providing an alternative deadline. Once she's said her piece, however, it's locked and loaded and she owns the task of getting it done on time and in good shape.

12. *Maintain written record of the meeting (the Minutes).*

The Minutes document summarizes what was stated and decided upon during the course of the meeting. You can have a regularly assigned Minute taker but, in all fairness, it would be a good idea to switch off this role in order to avoid burdening any one individual. The individual who handles the Minutes should prepare the document in the exact same format as prior minute takers. This is common sense, after all; if every set of Minutes looks different, it would take extra time for people to process the information within them.

When the meeting is done, circulate the approved Minutes document to all team members as soon as possible. Copies of all the Minutes should be stored in chronological order (with the dates in the respective titles) in a central shared server all team members can access. It is recommended that, at the beginning of the next meeting, a representative read a quick summary of these meeting Minutes to refresh everyone's memory and to ensure action items have been completed.

The above Goal and Control Checklist may seem like a lot of formality, but it's imperative to follow it each and every time. Mark my words: The one occasion it's not handled to the letter will be the one time something tragic slips through the cracks. It's also all too easy to get lazy; if the Checklist is missed at one meeting, it becomes "ok" to skip it the next time with the sentiment "Oh, we did fine last time without it." In my view, that is playing with fire—and risks jeopardizing an entire project, if not the company's topline goals for the year as well.

Parrot the Pareto Principle

There is a universal concept known as "the Pareto Principle," which was named after its originator, Italian economist Vilfredo Pareto. Although the original philosophy related to land ownership in Italy, it can be applied to a wide range of subjects.

Essentially, the Pareto Principle dictates that you: "Concentrate on the vital few; ignore the trivial many." In other words, 80% of a problem is often caused by 20% of the contributing factors. The ultimate goal of being in business is not just the pursuit of sales or profits or even cash. Yes, those things are important. But it's far more sensible to focus on what is maximizing (or depreciating) the value of the business over the long-term. You want to increase the elements that improve business performance with the least amount of oppositional current, mistakes, and overall loss.

That said, one size does not fit all. The value of a business is directly tied to the size, predictability, sustainability, and growth rate of earnings and how well human capital is being managed within the organization. If you don't have the *right* people focused on the *right* things following the *right* directives, you are not going to meet your desired level of success.

Measuring Success for the Community

Ah, now we get to my favorite part: determining whether the QOF is making a difference not only with the QOZB, but to the QOZ community as well. This is much trickier to assess than the other measurables, but it is equally as important—if not more so. Ideally, you would want to set a high bar right out of the gate, such as: *Can unemployment in the QOZ be cut in half in thirty-six months?*

If you have community members on the Board of Directors (or Advisory Board), it is recommended that they be granted sufficient time slotted on each meeting agenda to provide available statistics, insights, and commentary on how the QOZ has been faring. Let's keep in mind, however, that it's easy for progress to be derailed by regulations (see Chapter Fifteen for my thoughts on how to address this), area bureaucracy, and politics. Do not let this in any way discourage you. You must stand vigilant.

The main point of discussion should surround the trending economic status of the QOZ with mention of continuing and new roadblocks and how they are being addressed. Resources should be devoted to helping the community Board members provide regular deep dives into the state of affairs for the QOZ. As stated earlier, the most important yardstick for success is how many baby steps have been taken. As Robert Kiyosaki (author of *Rich Dad, Poor Dad*) once said, "Remember to dream big, think long-term, underachieve on a daily basis, and take baby steps. That is the key to long-term success."

If a QOZ's economy and unemployment rate had been perpetually dipping for years but remained flat or improved by as much as even 5%

within a cycle, that is cause for celebration. It all must be put in perspective in terms of the reality of the QOZs: *where it was, where it is now, how far it has come, and where it ultimately will be.*

These are the questions that should be asked:

1. How many people in the community have the QOF investment employed vs. the goal?
2. Has the QOF moved the needle to improve the overall employment rate in the community vs. the goal?
3. Has the average household income improved in the QOZ vs. the goal?
4. Have new investors supported the QOF?
5. Are new QOFs being invested in the QOZ?
6. What other areas of the community have been improved (i.e., infrastructure, crime rate, drug rate, etc.)?

There are also some intangibles that simply can't be measured, which is why you want Board members from the community to share anecdotes and observations that help paint a picture of the positive things that have been happening in the area. These examples aren't necessarily numbers-oriented, but they can be *seen* and *felt* and provide inspiration and motivation for everyone involved. These are some of the types of things you would take great pride in hearing:

- *The other day, over a half dozen teens were playing basketball in the restored court in the park.*

- *The mayor feels the downtown area has improved so much she is lobbying to bring back the Memorial Day Parade.*

- *My wife and I had a delicious dinner the other night at a new Indian restaurant in a building that used to be a pawnshop.*

- *I heard several people tell me how excited they are that we're finally going to have a new movie theater in town.*

- *It occurred to me while driving on Main Street that my tire didn't hit that same pothole again. It's been filled and I won't get another flat.*

- *I heard that a QOF is funding a low-cost daycare center—I can't wait to bring my little baby Maggie there!*

Like I said, baby steps!

In Closing . . . Let's Close the Books

Although specific goals and projects may be on varied calendar meeting schedules, the overall "state of business affairs" must be discussed on a continuous basis as follows:

- **Mid-Month Review:** This meeting is held no later than the 15th of each month. The intent is to: monitor the progress toward achieving the current month's financial goals; make course corrections, if necessary; and begin establishing the goals for the following month.

- **Monthly Review:** Most businesses close up the books at the end of the month. Finance usually requires a few days after that to process the information and run their reports. At some point within the first week of the following month, the financials should be ready for the Monthly Review. At this time, the leadership team discusses where the organization stands for the month vs. the plan and also the trajectory for the remainder of the year. If the month is running over in revenue and/or profit, balloons and confetti fill the room. (I'm just kidding—it's way too early for that. However, it's always good for the leadership team to pause and reflect on a good month.)

    If the month is short on revenue or profit, then the relevant parties must explain the shortfalls and identify whether it's bad timing (such as with an expected payment), a negative trend, and how the gap will be made up the following month.

- **Quarterly Review:** These are obviously more intense as you reach the third and fourth quarters. "Making the quarter" in terms of revenue and/or profit is essential, and once again, you have to see whether a trend above or below the goal is a one-time occurrence or the forming of a downtrending pattern. The further the year progresses, the more serious quarterly gaps become and action steps must be taken to improve the business.

- **Annual End of Year Review:** This is the biggie. All stones are overturned to determine what went right and what went wrong in the budget and with regard to expected earnings. Was it a matter of poor forecasting—or did unexpected events occur one way or the other? The leadership team must take ownership and be held accountable when shortfalls occur. On the opposite end, the organization as a whole receives widespread praise when financial targets are met and goals have been accomplished. This is a shared success.

- **Offsite:** I recommend that leadership teams meet offsite for a day or two no later than October 31st of each year to set the following year's budget and operating plans. At this time, adjustments can be made to update the five-year plan.

- **The Final Budget:** The budget and operating plans for the upcoming year should be finalized and ready for review and approval no later than December 15th. At this juncture, staffing, capital improvement, and acquisition plans are also discussed and given stamps of approval.

As you no doubt have deduced by now, measuring a QOZB's success is not an easy matter. The main guiding principle for you is to lead, guide, mentor, coach, and pay attention to the business drivers during all of the proper established checkpoints. You need to pay enough attention to know what is going on and offer to assist when needed but, outside of that, it's your main responsibility to *get out of the way and let people do what they are being paid to do*. You will be amazed at how well the team performs when afforded enough space and creative freedom.

As for investors…well, that's an entirely different matter. They need you to instill confidence that you and your team have things under control and that the business is in safe, capable hands. Mostly, of course, they want to know how their pockets will be impacted by the state of the business. In order to accomplish this, you need to be transparent, communicative, and forthcoming with topline facts and anticipated answers to their most pressing questions. An iron gut is usually helpful for these discussions. No need to worry, however. In Chapter Thirteen, Ole' Doc White has a powerful antacid remedy that can get you through even the most challenging investor relationships.

CHAPTER THIRTEEN

BUILDING CONFIDENT INVESTORS

If you have been following the progression of the last few chapters and implementing the Circle of Success, you are already well ahead of the game toward having a strong and favorable position with your investors. Doc White has provided you with powerful medicine to keep your company safe and healthy for both the short- and long-terms.

That's not to say you are immune from the same dangers that might potentially impact any company at any time. The good news is that I have another preventive prescription to help investors feel secure about how you are managing your QOZB—no matter what storm might be headed your way.

I readily admit that building confident investor relationships requires *a great deal of continuous work*. However, it's worth the enormous effort. By following my advice in this chapter on a consistent basis, you will be inoculated against potential investor flare-ups.

What Keeps Investors Up at Night?

Investors looking to make money on capital gains savings are a pretty sophisticated bunch. They aren't neophytes, having "been there, done that" and having "seen it all" in the investment world. They aren't just looking at your company's performance and the return on their investment—both of which are hugely important, of course—they are also paying attention to the emerging threats that may happen one, two, three, or even ten years down the line. These are just a few of the emerging potential threats:

- The value of the dollar.

- Rising interest rates.

- U.S. policies and regulations.

- The political climate.

- Recession.

- Impact of technology that makes your product or service obsolete.

Question: What do all of the above threats have in common?
Answer: They are all beyond your control.

Naturally, no one is able to control what is uncontrollable. However, you *can* control the following:

- The strength of your management team.

- The frequency and quality of your communications to investors.

- The steps you are taking to combat current threats.

- Your company's preparation against future threats.

Once you understand how to stay on top of these controllable elements, you will have built powerful relationships with your investors. All of this knowledge will go a long way toward sustaining you and the QOZB when you require more investor resources or are battling against strong headwinds.

Are You Experienced?

The first thing investors are looking for is an experienced management team that has a significant portfolio of credentials. They want to see evidence that the CEO and the senior team have a measurable track record of successes in this specific industry. They want and expect that the best, most qualified people are running the organization and can handle anything that might come their way. The business needs to run profitably, whether there is an economic downturn or not. You have to be able to show investors that your team can recover from such circumstances faster than competitive company leaders.

Upfront, investors will ask two questions about company leadership: "Who are you?" and "Why should I care?" Looking at the tenure of each specific individual, an investor may also ask, "Have you managed during tough economic times?"

In translation, all of this means that you can't afford to take a chance on having inexperienced leaders running the QOZB—even if you want to give someone talented and earnest a chance. Capital gains investors will sniff out inexperience and, once they do, they will have some doubt about the future of the business every step of the way. On the other hand, if you have experienced talent at the helm, they will have greater trust that the ship is being run smoothly.

Can You Clearly State Your Business Model?

Ideally, your company's business model is as airtight as a powerhouse elevator pitch. It must be clear, concise, and easily understood. If your model is "too complicated" and requires a lot of explanation, investors will be wary and/or too intimidated to invest in it. Creating a good business model is an art form that often requires "making the invisible *visible*."

No matter how high tech or complex a business might be, your task is to summarize it in the most simple, appealing terms possible. It could be the best new app in the world, but if the business model summary is too technical, takes too long to describe, or solves an unclear want or need, you will have lost the attention of investors. Here are a few excellent sample business model summaries, which also occasionally overlap with company Mission:

- **Facebook (original model):** "An expanding online directory that connects students, alumni, faculty, and staff through social networks at colleges and universities. This online directory allows for user connections on the basis of friendship, courses, and social networks (including intra and inter-school networks) and has a built-in messaging system."

- **Buzzfeed:** "One stop shop for web buzz: Editorial, Algorithmic, User Generated."

- **Foursquare:** "Think: part friend-finder, part social-city guide, part social guide. Foursquare is a mobile application that helps you keep up with your friends while using game mechanics to encourage and reward users for experiencing new things."

- **Google:** "...to organize the world's information and make it universally accessible and useful. Today, people around the world turn to Search to find information, learn about topics of interest, and make important decisions. We consider it a privilege to be able to help. As technology continues to evolve, our commitment will always be the same: helping everyone find the information they need."

- **Lowe's:** "Together, deliver the right home improvement products, with the best service and value, across every channel and community we serve."

- **Dollar General:** "Dollar General Corporation has been delivering value to shoppers for 80 years through its mission of *Serving Others*. Dollar General helps shoppers Save time. Save money. Every day!® by offering products that are frequently used and replenished, such as food, snacks, health and beauty aids, cleaning supplies, basic apparel, housewares and seasonal items at everyday low prices in convenient neighborhood locations...."

Note that in all of the above cases, the companies are structured around their business models in every way—including how they address marketing, branding, customer interaction, and even internal employee oversight. Google, for example, has such a brilliant business model that most people between the ages of ten and eighty—unless they've been under a rock in a deep cave—know exactly what is meant when someone says "Google it" to find a piece of information.

Think Visual

Business models are often supplemented with diagram representations of the business in action. People love pictures—as long as the diagram is as easy-to-follow as the written business model statement itself. You should be able to look at the diagram and decipher it in the blink of an eye.

Along with the diagram, you would want to provide a concise, explanatory narrative that is equally as digestible. From just a quick review, investors need to see and understand how the cash and capital flow through your business model. They are always looking to determine how well your business "stacks up" as a company: Proof of revenue sources is an excellent way to earn investor confidence.

I've also learned over the years through trial and error that all of the following plans must tie in with the business model: strategy, operations, staffing, sales/marketing, and so on. The implementation and execution in all of these areas must exemplify the business model in action. If something is out of sync—such as a poor retailer discount by a company that states its model is based on competitive pricing—investors will lose faith and think the entire business is flawed.

BUSINESS MODEL

Leave No Stone Unturned and No Question Unanswered

In addition to an experienced team and an airtight and straightforward business model, investors are also looking for you to have answers about the business at the ready. If you aren't knowledgeable and prepared as needed, investor confidence starts to ebb.

These are four of the main questions investors might ask you at any time:

1. *What are your strategic goals and priorities?* These should be boiled down to just the top three-to-five that impact the entire business, not just one segment.
2. *How will you achieve your goals and priorities?* You need to present a credible step-by-step plan for accomplishing each goal and priority.
3. *How far have you progressed against these goals and priorities?* Investors must always see tangible, quantifiable progress.
4. *How are you in terms of positioning the company in the wider market?* Investors' ears will always perk up when you are able to pinpoint areas of opportunity, expansion, and growth.

Of course, a startup business is different in terms of investor expectations. Investors know and understand that it will take time for things to come together in a new business—especially for a QOZB. Even so, over time they will look to see some progress towards achieving the goals out of the gate, even if they are just baby steps.

It's Risky Business to Avoid Citing Risk

Not all investors are the same in terms of their tolerance to risk; some have a high threshold, whereas others don't. Your best bet is to assume the former and hope for the latter. In other words, no matter how daunting the risk factors might be, you must specifically provide a full and cogent description of all risk factors with as much information as possible in terms of the "likelihood" these events will occur.

There is no benefit to "protecting" investors from risk factors. The phrase "What they don't know can't hurt them" is false. You won't be saving them sleepless nights by concealing the risks. The fact is, investors don't like surprises. This is a big deal: If you fail to mention a risk factor to your business and it comes to pass, harming your progress toward achieving goals—watch out! Your investors will lose trust and faith in your ability to manage the business.

You may have heard the phrase KPIs—Key Performance Indicators—at one time or another. In simple terms, these are the main performance areas for your specific business. They may not be the same from one business to the next—or at least be in the same order of priority. For your business, you must identify the KPIs and how they link back to the core of your business, including to the company's remuneration policy.

Some major KPIs include:

• Revenue Growth.

• Net Profit Margin.

• Gross Profit Margin.

• Operational Cash Flow.

• Current Accounts Receivables.

• Inventory Turnover.

• EBITDA.

You may also have additional KPIs within specific areas of your business that impact the company has a whole. For example, in Sales you might have a KPI for the specific amount of revenue you expect will be generated by a single account. If that particular customer is in danger of closing stores or potentially even going out of business, the revenue target is a major at risk KPI—a fact that needs to be conveyed to investors.

The upshot is that you must be prepared to identify and explain risks to your company's KPIs and what you intend to do to mitigate them in case they occur. If, for example, a major account shuts down stores, several Dominoes might collapse: they may reduce their orders; they might be unable to pay their bills on time, if at all; they might return all stock of your product; etc.

What are you prepared to do to counter all of this fallout? Potential solutions might be: directing sales efforts to opening new channels and finding replacement customers; reducing production and inventory of the product ordered by that customer; or shifting priority to developing a product that is more suitable to an account that is on safer ground.

Let's take this several steps further. Every business I ever owned and/or operated addressed the question: *What will happen to the business if the economy falls apart?*

You would be amazed at how few companies prepare themselves for this obvious possibility. Not to be negative, but recessions have occurred time and time again in our country's history, and it's shameful when companies don't have a contingency plan for it. Over the years I have owned and run many companies, and I have always had a plan for economic downturns. Even if it doesn't happen—which is what we all hope for, of course—investors know that my businesses are safeguarded. This makes you golden in the eyes of investors, building immense trust for the present and the future.

There are a number of other things that can help instill trust among investors regarding risk factors. Back in Chapter Twelve, I presented the Goal and Control Report. I can't tell you how invaluable this Report is to investors and bankers who might be concerned about looming risks. They have come to understand that, if the business goals are being properly managed vs. targets, the direct impact of a calamitous event (such as a recession) is greatly reduced, if not avoided entirely.

Similarly, the twice a month accountability reviews add further reinforcement of your ability to oversee the business. They show you are on top of things. Through these two meetings, investors learn how close you are to the target and the steps you are taking to get there. If at any time an investor demands an update or an explanation for a specific detail of your strategic plan, you are well prepared with responses. It is unlikely your business will have a last-minute twelve-alarm fire and, if you do, you have extinguishers at the ready. I must reiterate: *No surprises!*

The following phrases should become your mantra (your responsibility is to fill in the blanks related to your business):

This is what we said we would do.

This is what we planned to do.

This is what we've done so far.

This is what we will do moving forward.

This is what we will do if x, y, and z go wrong.

Rinse and repeat: *I will communicate to my investors, I will communicate to my investors, I will communicate to my investors…*

How to Communicate—*Over-communicate!*

No matter what is happening with the business, I recommend erring on the side of over-communicating topline information. Investors may forget some of the details from one month to the next or seem indifferent to certain details, but be rest assured that the one thing you fail to message or clearly communicate will bite you in the you-know-what. If the information is in any way crucial to sustaining the business, you should report it—even if you wonder whether the investors are paying attention. When you have doubt about how well your message has registered, ask investors to repeat back to you what they heard.

I recommend that you communicate regularly to investors through a quarterly webcast that covers progress towards goals, KPIs, and risk factors (again, including what you are doing to protect the company). You'll want to email reports and documents and/or include screen shares of slides with specific backup information, including simple graphics and charts that illustrate key points.

It goes without saying that all emails, documents, reports, charts, and graphs must be incisive and appear in an easy-to-follow format. In other words, don't tell the entire story: Get straight to the point. Do not under any circumstances try to include art or graphics for the sake of humor: at the least this is distracting; at the most it is irritating and perhaps even offensive to someone.

The company's Annual Report is obviously a major endeavor, summarizing all of the financials and how the company fared versus goals for the year. A section in the Report should be devoted to the before-and-after impact of the QOF on the overall QOZ community, with updated statistics on population, employment, annual household earnings, and perhaps a few impactful headline bullets of tangible things that have been repaired and improved (i.e., areas of infrastructure).

Investors have different preferences for how they receive and process information, so you want to cover as many of them as possible. Your QOZB website is critical, as you never know when an investor desires information right at his or her fingertips and can't wait for the next web meeting. The site needs to be attractive, easily navigable, user-friendly, and be protected with secure logins reserved only for approved investors. The site should also be comprehensive and fully transparent. Anything reported at the meetings—financials, quarterly and annual reports, links to web meetings, etc.—should be downloadable and consistent in terms of messaging.

Presentation Matters

Last but not least, all of your presentations—whether on the phone, by video, or even in person—must be polished and professional with great respect paid to investors' investment of time and money. Patrick Riley of the Global Accelerator Network recommends several excellent ways to earn investor trust through strong presentations, which I've blended with some of my personal thinking:

- *Show up on time.* If you are late, you will have insulted your investors. Depending on their personalities and patience level—not to mention how late you are—this alone could cause you to lose significant investor confidence.

- *Don't get defensive if difficult questions are asked.* Investors will ask tricky questions. Some of them might sound aggressive to you or second-guess what you are doing. Smile and answer with authority, but do not get defensive. Stick with your strategies and your progress toward goals.

- *Keep your ego in check.* If investors offer advice and/or solutions, acknowledge it with grace. Take the wisdom at face value; he or she is trying to be helpful, not to embarrass you or run your business for you. You don't have to accept the advice or "one up" the investor to show how smart you are. Instead, recognize it with appreciation and get back to the investor with a well thought out and courteous response.

- *Follow-up well.* If there are follow-up questions or action items from investors, get back to them right away. Do not ever let them linger or skepticism and doubt will come into play.

- *Get to know the investors.* When possible, it's helpful if you find out some quick facts about the investor—backgrounds, areas of interest, commonalities, etc. The more you know, the easier it will be to communicate with him or her in the future.

- *Ask two questions upfront.* The questions could be about the agenda or regarding their expectations for the meeting. By inviting the investors to participate in the meeting early, you are engaging them right away and ensuring that they feel valued. The meeting will go better with fewer digressions from them because you have solicited their input upfront and made adjustments.

- *Never lie.* This is a biggie. It is virtually impossible to earn back trust if you are ever caught fibbing to investors. Ethics are important and nothing is worth sacrificing your reputation. You win investor confidence by earning their trust, even if it means conveying uncomfortable news.

- *Always believe in your Vision, Mission, Values, and Strategies.* No matter how things are faring in the business, it's important to stick to your guns about what you and the company stand for. Your passion and commitment to the company must prevail. If you don't wave the flag, who will?

Like I said at the beginning: All of this sounds like a lot of work, doesn't it? Yes—because it is! I'm not going to soft-soap the fact that it is *a great responsibility* to build and maintain investor confidence. I've seen many companies fail because they aren't doing the legwork for goal control and what it takes to ensure effective communication with investors.

Please feel free to quote me on this: *A well-informed investor is a happy investor!* Aside from the obvious reasons for wanting to have happy investors, there is also the possibility that you will want to woo them again for your next QOF venture. Unless you are nearing retirement, you want to keep your good karma going and contribute all you can toward improving QOZs. This means not stopping to rest on your laurels, but focusing your attention on finding the next logical Big Thing to add to your QOF portfolio of businesses.

CHAPTER FOURTEEN

FINDING THE NEXT BIG THING

The following is a famous unattributed quote that I hold near and dear: "The past cannot be changed. The future is in your power." Have you ever wondered what will be "the next big thing" for our world? Will it be colonizing Mars, flying hovercraft cars, or winding up robot butlers to answer our front doors?

In a brief time, we have come a long way from the light bulb, the transistor radio, and the phonograph. Consider these facts about progressive formats for commercial music products: cassette tapes didn't exist in 1950; CDs were not a possibility in 1970; and few imagined in 1990 that virtually every song you can think of would someday be available as digital downloads. It is only the limits of our current imaginations that prevent us from seeing what that next music format will be down the road—but eventually it will come—and probably sooner than you think. The delivery of music content is just one tiny example of accelerated technological change in a segment of the marketplace; there are many others I could provide, but I think you get the point.

This is how I visualize the future in terms of QOZs: One successful QOF will lead to another, which will lead to another, and so forth. When investment money starts to flow into QOZs and investors see employment rates improve and formerly depressed communities flourish, more people will begin to recognize that the benefits of QOZ legislation are endless. Invention and innovation will arise out of the ashes and have an opportunity to reign supreme in areas that, unfortunately, had been written off by large populations of people.

Beginning with Benjamin Franklin, one of our nation's founding fathers, America has always been at the forefront of invention and innovation. Sometimes I think we have become so embroiled in *using* our technology that we don't spend enough time taking pride in our rich history of men and women pioneers. We should be studying what these remarkable individuals accomplished in order to light the way for "the next big thing":

- **Benjamin Franklin:** the lightning rod, bifocal glasses, and the flexible urinary catheter. (Bet you didn't know that last one!)

- **Margaret E. Knight:** the paper bag. (Yes, believe it or not, this is a fact!)

- **Josephine Cochrane:** the mechanical dishwasher.

- **Thomas Edison:** the photograph and the incandescent electric light.

- **Alexander Graham Bell:** the telephone and the gramophone.

- **Nikola Tesla:** the alternating-current (AC) electric system.

- **The Wright Brothers:** the controls that revolutionized modern aircraft.

- **Albert Einstein:** the scientific foundation for products such as paper towels and lasers. (Of course, he also made a little discovery known as the Theory of Relativity, among numerous other significant accomplishments.)

- **Eli Whitney:** the cotton gin.

- **George Westinghouse:** the railway air brake.

- **George Washington Carver:** 300 products made from peanuts.

- **Henry Ford:** the model T car and the modern car production assembly line.

- **Mary Anderson:** windshield wipers.

- **Ruth Graves Wakefield:** the chocolate chip cookie. (Where would we be without this marvelous invention?)

- **Charles Goodyear:** the process of vulcanization leading to the creation of commercial rubber (used in car tires and other products).

- **Hedy Lamarr:** the concept of "frequency hopping" to encrypt torpedo signals that has led to the modern advent of GPS, WIFI, and Bluetooth (And yes, this is *the* Hedy Lamarr—the actress who lit up the silver screen in the 1940s and 50s.)

- **Bill Gates:** the programming for the first microcomputer.

- **Steve Jobs:** the Mac, the iPad, and the iPhone.

Who will be America's risk takers and geniuses of tomorrow and where will they be found? I firmly believe that QOFs will rekindle this innovative and entrepreneurial spirit in places you'd least expect—perhaps in a household garage located in the middle of a QOZ. Many remarkable individuals who went on to achieve great things started out in low-end garages: Walt and Roy Disney (creating cartoons); Bill Hewlett and Dave Packard (building the audio oscillator, HP's first major product); Larry Paige and Sergey Brin (starting Google). It's not farfetched to envision that—with the right people, money, resources, and encouragement in the form of QOFs—the next Steve Jobs or Bill Gates can have the means to labor in his or her garage and build something revolutionary that will change the world.

Why am I so confident about our bright future with QOFs? The answer is simple: In many cases, "the next big thing" is already becoming a reality.

Science Fiction Is Becoming Non-Fiction

Let's pause for one moment and reflect back on our thoughts from ten or twenty years ago. Did we truly believe robots, virtual reality, and self-driving cars would be a genuine possibility—or deep down think it was merely the stuff of science fiction stories and films? Yet here we are, firmly planted at a time during which manufacturing plants are being operated by robots; surgeons are performing procedures utilizing virtual reality; and Hyundai is investing $35 billion in self-driving automotive technology.

Some people might insist that: "Self-driving cars will never happen because they are too dangerous." Well, let's go back to the history. How many people originally believed the first airplanes would rise up and then just plummet from the sky? Today, airplanes are just another common mode of transportation, and we all seem perfectly comfortable taking naps in our seats while the craft is being placed on autopilot.

Not all that long ago, back in the mid-1990s, I recall a lot of people being afraid to make a book purchase on a then unknown startup website called Amazon.com because they didn't feel secure enough typing in their credit card numbers. For this reason and consumer affinity for brick-and-mortar retail shopping, many experts said this site and other consumer web businesses would sink like stones. Well, Amazon.com overcame that concern and is now *a $160 billion company*. In fact, I can't name a single person today who is "too afraid" to purchase a product on that juggernaut site, which now offers everything from books and music to food and pet care products to gardening tools and lounge chairs. Jeff Bezos never saw any limits to what his brainchild could offer in a virtual store, so why should you limit your thinking of what might be accomplished in a QOZ?

Below are just a few of the areas that are becoming a reality as we speak:

1. **Mobile payments:** Many of us already use apps to pay for our coffees at Starbucks and handle some of our banking transactions. It is not far-fetched to think that soon plastic credit cards will be discarded entirely in favor of mobile application payments.

2. **5G Networks:** If you can remember back to the first screechy and time-consuming "dial up" connections to the Internet, you will be stunned by the blazing speed connecting networks will soon have. Programmers are already developing online bandwidths from cellular networks that will enable lightning-fast connections and information downloads.

3. **Sustainable products:** These are all the rage and many are already available, including lamps that grow plants in windowless spaces; pineapple fibre leather to replace animal skin (handbags, sneakers, etc.); a reusable straw that removes water

contaminants; and even sturdy homes made from plastic bottles.

4. **Medical wearables:** We are only at the birth of what is possible with technology (such as the Apple Watch) that can monitor health. Soon we will have tracking and healing devices for a range of illnesses and maladies—and even ones for pets.

5. **Drones:** We know these have been weaponized by the military and put to other uses that usually involve some sort of spying. Looking forward, drones are going to revolutionize commercial and personal photography, video, and filmmaking, as these devices can explore images and angles that were previously unattainable.

6. **Biofuels:** Biofuels, which are obviously much better for our environment than fossil fuels, have already been in usage and, over time, will ultimately take precedence.

7. **Screens:** Computer monitors and TV screens are becoming slimmer and slimmer; soon they will be paper-thin.

8. **Universal translators:** Imagine traveling to another country and being addressed in a foreign language. Well, there will be an app for that! In the near future, you will have the capability of translating international languages into English with the click of a button.

The above are by no means the end of all the amazing things to come. They are just a representative sample to provide a frame of reference and, hopefully, some inspiration to help you think out of the box with your QOFs.

Aesop Wrote Truth—Not Just Fables

The ancient Greek storyteller Aesop is often given credit for the following quote: "Your level of success is only limited by your imagination."

How is it possible that someone who lived so many centuries ago could have conceived a statement so profound and relevant today? And yet...Aesop did. In order to accomplish great things, we must begin with great imaginations. All of the most celebrated artists in world history from Shakespeare to Picasso to The Beatles started out being inspired by the past to create a whole new unexpected future in their respective artistic areas.

This is exactly what we need to do in QOZs: We must believe that everyone has the potential to exceed expectations and contribute something wonderful for the company, the community, and our country. I maintain that a complete rebirth is attainable in America—not necessarily in the cities that are already thriving and profiting, but in the underdog rural and urban QOZs that only require some QOF resources and a little bit of faith. Despite the tragic polarization that is happening in our country, I believe we remain capable of boosting the American spirit *for everyone* by creating a foundation for success in these previously neglected areas.

There is nothing from preventing you, as a savvy QOF investor, from sparking innovation in any area you choose and placing it in a QOZ. Imagine the story you will have to tell if your QOF in, for example, Cuyahoga County—the census tract with the highest poverty rate in the state of Ohio at a staggering 86.7%—were to house a QOZB with the largest factory in the world that produces drones for private and commercial use? This is not a flight of fancy or fable, if you will.

Real estate may be the low-hanging fruit for QOF investments, but the real opportunities should only start there. The possibilities are endless within this and other areas:

- Agriculture.

- Architecture.

- Arts and Entertainment.

- Athletic Centers.

- Banks and Other Financial Institutions.

- Brick-and-Mortar Retail.

- Crafts.

- Criminal and Social Justice.

- Day Care Centers.

- Education.

- Energy.

- Entertainment Centers.

- Exploration. (Yes, even dreams of underwater exploration and venturing into outer space should be considered.)

- Food Service and Restaurants.

- Health Care.

- Home and Land Maintenance and Repair.

- Infrastructure.

- Manufacturing Plants.

- Medical Care and Medicine.

- Non-Profits.

- Online Products and Services.

- Professional Services.

- Science.

- Technology.

- Warehouses and Storage Facilities.

- Wholesalers.

The above list is just the tip of the iceberg. Someday, it is my sincere hope I live to see the day when the world's greatest minds rise from QOZs and win Nobel Prizes in Literature, Science, Mathematics, and so forth. In addition, I would like to see other individuals from QOZs become the next generation of politicians and leaders to fight for even better legislation than what appears in the 2017 tax bill. I would be equally as thrilled to witness some previously unemployed QOZ residents emerge as millionaires and billionaires themselves. This is the United States, after all, and we are here to live the American Dream—which, in my view, is a future reality—not a pipe dream.

I'd love nothing more than to close this chapter and Part Four of this book with the above uplifting sentiment, but there is one more crucial area left for us to cover: rules and regulations that may become barriers to growing and maximizing your QOF investments and dreams of invention and innovation. These matters can prove to be major nuisances, but they should not discourage you from enthusiastically charging full steam ahead—especially since you have Doc White standing right by your side to help swat away anything blocking your path.

PART FIVE

OVERCOMING BARRIERS TO GROWTH

CHAPTER FIFTEEN

STREAMLINING RULES AND REGULATIONS

Welcome to the fifth and final part of our journey into mining QOF investment opportunities in QOZs. There is rich quarry to be unearthed and developed for everyone concerned—communities, residents, workers and, of course, investors—but, as with all good things, you must exert sufficient elbow grease and substantial legwork to extract the gold nuggets and be in a position to share the rewards. Once all of that labor has been completed and you can visualize your "next big thing" within your grasp, one sole attribute is necessary above all others: *patience.*

When you, as an investor, come to realize a capital gains advantage, you have 180 days to decide what to do with it: 1) pay the IRS or 2) invest it in a fund (i.e., QOF). During that vital period of time when you are looking to do the latter, you need your QOZB concept—whether you are starting a business or improving an existing one—to be "shovel ready" for deployment, so you can take immediate action. With the assistance of your team of experts, you file all of the paperwork for the town, city, country, or state municipality as cleanly as possible while following all of the specified instructions to the letter. Then you wait…and wait…and wait.

"What is the holdup?" you are no doubt asking.

Call it what you will—paper shuffling, red tape, or bureaucracy—it is the one thing that may stand in your way and cause unnecessary delays and frustrations to capitalizing on your QOFs. This is not a reflection of the good people who work hard and do their best in these municipalities. In many cases, unfortunately, their hands are tied. In addition to being under-staffed to handle the volume of paperwork that flows through their offices, the processes, reviews, rules, regulations, and signoffs can often be so burdensome, complicated, and time-consuming that they can take two years to fully execute—sometimes, as I've learned, even up to four.

For a QOF funding a start-up or business improvement, there could be innumerable forms that require completion, processing, and approval. Every municipality has its own set of regulations for land use, housing, building, infrastructure, and other areas—not to mention zoning and work permit laws.

In some instances, as I've personally discovered, one minor inadvertent typo or missed line could mean that the paperwork sits in someone's box for *a really long time* before someone in the office decides to return the entire application packet by snail mail with a "REJECT" stamp on it. Guess what happens then? You have to make the correction, resubmit it into the chain, and the clock starts all over again from the beginning. The regulators typically have thirty days to review the revision (it may vary from one municipality to the next); hopefully, everything is clean and they don't find another mistake that should have been caught the first time.

This is not acceptable in any way, shape, or form! We can't allow this to happen if we want the QOZ initiative to be successful and achieve its full potential. We need and want to see as many "next big things" coming to fruition as possible.

Okay, Doc White has vented his piece. I will now let my cool head prevail as I explain what must be done to remedy the burdensome red tape issue and streamline the process. First, let's delve into what *should not* be done.

Many Regulations Do Matter

When I talk about streamlining regulations, I'm not suggesting for one split-second that we should do away with smart regulations that are protections for the people of the community. Without firm rules and regulations in place and enforced, terrible outcomes are possible: the tap water people consume could be contaminated; building foundations not up to code could collapse a year later; the air in the region could be polluted with harmful toxins; and so forth.

These and many other good rules and regulations are in place for genuine public safety reasons and cannot ever be compromised. On the other hand, I *do* suggest that we squash unnecessary regulations that don't make any sense whatsoever, yet have been on the books for over a century because people gloss over them, don't want to rock the boat, it's too much trouble, or are simply afraid of change because "it's always been that way."

It all comes down to common sense and what works to protect the people, the community, and the environment from genuine threats that might actually occur *today*.

Time to Get to Work

If you haven't surmised by now, what *I am* most opposed to is *wasted time*. Your time as an investor, business owner, and/or entrepreneur is far too valuable a commodity to waste—and these communities don't have a second to spare.

In order to bring momentum to your QOF-funded projects and make time your ally, you need to roll up your sleeves once again and spread Doc White's message about the many benefits of QOZ legislation.

Research, Research, Research
The first thing you need to do is learn about the community and the people you'll be working with. You must conduct research in order to be informed about the following areas of the community:

- Its rich history.

- Its main problem areas.

- Its recent accomplishments.

- Its leadership: strengths, weaknesses, and interests.

- Its areas of potential opportunities.

- Its knowledge of prior efforts with QOFs in the QOZ, if any:

    - Do they seem to be working?

    - What setbacks have they faced?

Once you know more about the community, its leaders, and its history, you'll be well positioned to initiate the education process.

The School Bell Is Ringing

Your second order of business is *education*. Prior to—or at least simultaneous with—filling out all of that messy paperwork, you must educate the town, county, or state municipalities (whichever ones are applicable) about the goals of QOZ legislation and the specific benefits of QOF investments to their respective community.

I can assure you that one or more of these three circumstances exist with regard to QOZs:

1. The leaders, regulators, and public service workers don't know about the legislation or, if they do, don't understand it and can't be bothered with trying to figure it out.
2. They *think* they understand it, but are erroneously convinced that it's too politically charged to get involved.
3. They are *certain* they understand it (when they don't) and believe the legislation was put in place solely to make the rich even richer.

Since you now know a few key things about the community, you are well prepared to meet with its people at every level and take them through the ins and outs of QOFs in QOZs. Assume they are starting with a clean slate and know nothing about them. The simplest thing to do is hand them each a physical copy of the book you are holding in your hands. I know, that sounds like a shameless plug for me to sell more copies of *Opportunity Investing*. While I'd like nothing more than this to occur, my intent is not to milk book sales; rather, I recommend it because all of the tools anyone needs to understand QOZs are right here within these very pages.

Of course, giving everyone a book doesn't mean they'll actually read it or develop the sense of urgency that is necessary for QOF paperwork to flow smoothly through their bureaucracies. Therefore, we move on to the next line of offense:

1. *Private meetings with officials and community leaders:* These could be by phone or videoconference, but the most effective route is the personal touch. You can set up a brief meeting in their offices or perhaps even invite them for a coffee or lunch at the location of their choosing. During these discussions,

you are laying out the A to Zs of QOZs and tying them specifically to the needs of their community. How will the funds lead to job creation, higher wages, increased population, area improvements, and so on?

2. *Call a town hall with private citizens:* Invite the entire community to a town hall meeting where you take everyone step-by-step through the benefits of QOZ legislation and answer questions and concerns. When you do, steer clear of any and all political agendas. This is a *bipartisan effort* and the only thing that matters is the overall health of their community. In order for the effort to gain any traction whatsoever, the residents must understand QOZ legislation, put aside political biases, and fully embrace the concept.

3. *Reinforce the message:* Whenever possible, meet separately with the regulators, members of the relevant committees and planning commissions, and public service workers.

Now that you have everyone's attention and there is a complete communal understanding of the intentions behind the QOZ initiative as well as its many benefits, you are ready to bring out the heavy artillery.

Streamline!

Before Federal Express became the world's fastest courier service, one organization pretty much held the monopoly on mail delivery in this country for years: The United States Postal Service. But online businesses needed packages delivered faster than the post office could accommodate, given its limited budget and resources; bureaucratic structure and policies; and general years of malaise. With email and texting capabilities replacing "snail mail" for correspondence and direct mail marketing efforts, post office earnings plummeted and the antiquated institution seemed doomed.

Eventually, though, the sluggish wheels churned forward and the post office system started to revamp their business model and make some noticeable improvements. Not only do stamps no longer have to be licked (yuck, all of those germs!), it has now become possible to send a package for next day (or second day, etc.) arrival through Priority Mail; they can also print labels online, track packages, and so forth. In many cases, the post office options are a lot more economical—yet comparably reliable, efficient, and speedy—as the private carrier services.

Please don't misunderstand my intention here: This is not a commercial for the U.S. Post Office; nor am I trying to take down its competitors. I bring this up as an obvious example of how it's *possible* for even the most ancient, belabored bureaucracy to be overhauled and streamlined.

How do I know all of this is possible in rural and urban communities? Without citing specific locations in order to protect the innocent: I have successfully consulted with several municipalities to help them discover "the magic sauce" to simplifying all stages of their work using the Circle of Success program outlined in previous chapters. It's unlikely you will be able to impart COS to them, but you can still make a major difference in helping them simplify and accelerate their processes.

If you have already met with the municipalities and educated them about QOFs in their QOZs, the next step is to connect their hearts and heads with the initiative to ensure they understand the sense of urgency. See if you can hone in on the main pain points of the community and how QOFs will lead to resolving those issues. For example, if the area has a severe problem with affordable housing availability for its residents, cite how the QOFs can help resolve this crisis. Mention any and all financial upsides to the community from QOF investments. Assure them that you are not in any way attempting to do away with any regulations that are on the books for good reasons to safeguard the community. Conclude by emphasizing that these opportunities are only possible if their approval process is streamlined and efficient, and if the paperwork is given top priority amongst their stacks.

There may be pushback, protest, or even just plain indifference to your efforts. If this is the case, ask them what you can do to make it easier for them to process the paperwork prior to turning it all in. Find out what issues gum up and slow down the works. There may be something controllable on your end, such as avoiding a commonly made error on one of the forms.

Once you have turned in the paperwork, follow up politely and respectfully. Try to find out the source of the holdup and if there is anything you can do to help. Remind the regulators and public servant workers of what you had imparted to them in your earlier discussions about the importance of QOFs in QOZs. If you have established a solid relationship with these individuals and you are always charming in your dealings with them, they will be receptive to your follow-ups, appreciate your persistence and, hopefully, begin to follow your passion.

Once or twice a year you can hold a town meeting updating the community about progress with the QOFs. At this time, you can mention any success stories that might inspire individuals to move things along even faster on paperwork that is stuck in limbo. You can gently mention the holdups, but never point a finger or blame anyone as this could backfire on you and someone might sit on the paperwork just for the sake of being spiteful (not that I've ever actually experienced anyone doing this).

In summary: Your goodwill and respect to the leaders, regulators, and public servants will go a long way toward greasing the wheels and speeding up the approval process. At the end of the day, your passion and earned trust will make all the difference. And, once you have gone through this process in a QOZ, you have a model that can perhaps be even further streamlined with the "next big idea" you propose with your QOF investments in that same area.

Sadly (at least from my perspective), we are now heading toward the final chapter of this book. I thought it fitting that I bring all of the elements together with an important mini-instructional manual exploring a crucial subject that often gets short shrift: *the art of compromise.* If we don't find ways in the United States to know how and when to "agree to disagree" and "meet in the middle," we will not live up to expectations as being the world's greatest democracy. QOF investments in QOZs are the ideal place to put our political differences aside and create a path that allows opportunity for equal success for all people in the land of the free and the home of the brave.

CHAPTER SIXTEEN

DISCOVERING WAYS TO COMPROMISE

Colin Powell once said, "But just as they did in Philadelphia when they were writing the Constitution, sooner or later, you've got to compromise. You've got to start making the compromises that arrive at a consensus and move the country forward."

I couldn't agree more with that statement. If our Founding Fathers—who certainly disagreed on many things—hadn't come to an agreement on the principles of government, the United States of America wouldn't exist today.

I sometimes scratch my head and wonder why the "art of the compromise" has become such a lost art since colonial times. I figure that it's probably because people are out way too much to "win" and "win *big*"—meaning, everything must be on their own terms. It's "all or nothing" or there is no deal; be prepared to "walk away," they say. With this mindset, no matter what the outcome, it's lose-lose for all parties involved.

The fact of the matter is this: If we cannot come to a compromise, we have done a poor job. This doesn't just hold true in business and politics. We negotiate every day at work and in our family lives, yet often become too stubborn and fail to compromise in those areas as well.

Perhaps some of the failure resides in a misunderstanding of the meaning behind the word *compromise*. A lot of people think the word means you have given up something important to keep the peace. Rather than accept this type of thinking, I would suggest focusing on the positive and the mutual end result of the negotiation: *the solution*.

I define compromise along the lines of the following: "An ability to listen to two sides in a disagreement or dispute, concede points on both sides, and arrive at an amicable agreement that satisfies both parties in order to achieve a common goal." The above definition accentuates the positive aspects of compromise, not the negative possible connotation of *having been compromised.* It also ensures that all parties have a stated common goal. I believe this is always going to be the case; somehow, some way there is always a common goal. If both parties start with that and then backtrack, the question of "How do we get there?" becomes a lot easier.

I believe that all readers of this book—no matter which side of the political fence they are on—agree on at least one or more of the following points:

1. Every American citizen deserves an opportunity to succeed and achieve the American Dream.
2. Our economy and strength as a nation will improve if QOZs improve.
3. Every urban and rural community, including QOZs, deserves the opportunity to have increased job growth, soaring populations, higher earnings, reduced drugs and crime, and solid infrastructure that can serve as a model for the rest of the world.

Republican, Democrat, Independent, and every party in between must agree with at least one of the above statements, if not all three. With that in mind, it should be easy to backtrack from there and begin to compromise.

The only problem? Most people don't know *how* to compromise—even if they truly believe they are in the process of doing it. I would suggest that all of these thoughts get placed on the sidelines before sitting at the table and starting to have the conversation:

- *The Tax Bill is a scheme to make the rich richer, so I don't want anything to do with it.*

- *Capital gains advantages are just another capitalistic scheme to bilk the tax system.*

- *I can't stand the current Presidential administration, so I'm not going to admit there is something in the Tax Bill that makes sense and does some good for people.*

- *The people in rural and urban distressed communities already have the same opportunities as people everywhere else, so they should help themselves find ways to improve their neighborhoods.*

- *You'll never be able to get people to agree, so why even bother?*

Once you've tossed all of those statements right out the window, you are ready to come to the table and help further the cause for QOZs. While doing so, of course, you need to demonstrate what I call "Communication Norms" in order for your position of compromise to be effective.

Listen Is an Action Verb

Many business and political disagreements go sideways for the same reasons: the individuals don't know how to engage and speak with each other in civil tones; they allow their emotions to override their intellects and speech patterns; they fail to step into the shoes of the opposing viewpoint in order to understand it; and, most of all, they don't *listen*. In any conversation, you must take the time to allow other people to express their opinions without interruption. You need to listen carefully and make sure that you have fully understood what the person has said before you respond with a single word.

The dilemma then becomes the following: You *think* you know what the other person means—but do you really? How can you be so sure? And, even if you *do* fully comprehend what the other individual is conveying, how do you get that across in a sympathetic and authentic manner?

Human resource professionals often recommend mastering the art of *active listening*. Put simply, this is a way to demonstrate that you have *heard* and *understood* what the other person has said.

The skill requires that you interpret the speaker's words in the form of a question, so you don't give the impression that you have it 100% right. The reason for this is simple avoidance of presumption. Suppose, for example, you state: "I get it. You are saying that the regulations are too challenging to make investing your QOF in the QOZ worth your time."

How do you think the other party might react to that? I can safely tell you it would be something along the lines of, "[*Insert expletive here*] no! That isn't what I meant at all! Did you hear a word I said?"

On the other hand, phrasing your words as a question shows respect and places the onus on the other person to be clear about what she means. The response would be something along the lines of this: "I *hear* what you are saying—but I want to be sure I have it right. Do you mean to say that you believe the regulations will be a challenge for you? If that's the case, I might be able to help you figure them out."

In the above example, not only has the speaker acknowledged the other person's words and attempted to clarify meaning with a touch of empathy, she has taken it a step further by offering assistance. A couple of cautionary notes on that last point: you want to be 100% certain the other person isn't overly sensitive and won't interpret your suggestion as some sort of insult against her knowledge or ability; and you have to be prepared to deliver the goods on your promise to help if she comes back and takes you up on it. If the other party politely declines your assistance, do not be offended; simply smile and continue the dialogue.

Active listening also requires the right body language. Good eye contact and sitting upright are important, as is having a pleasant expression. If you raise your eyebrows, roll your eyes, slouch, yawn, sigh repeatedly, fidget in your chair, rap on the table, shuffle papers, check your watch ten times, or give any kind of impression that you don't want to be present, you have sucked away any positive impact of your active listening effort.

This also bears attention: I don't care how good you think you are at multi-tasking, it's just plain rude to be gazing at your phone or laptop while the other person is speaking. One would think this is obvious politeness and professionalism, but these days device addiction is so prevalent and distracting it's a wonder humans ever grasp anything said right in front of them.

Seven Additional Rules of Engagement

Active listening isn't the only tool in your toolbox. Compromise also requires that you follow these seven rules of engagement:

1. *Never go in with your mind made up.* In their classic book on negotiation *Getting to Yes*, authors Roger Fisher and William Ury state: "An open mind is not an empty one." If you have an open mind as you practice active listening, you might find that you agree with one or two points made by the other party. That is a *good* thing. It provides you with areas you can concede to add balance against the places where you can't. It takes a big person to see another person's point of view enough to change her mind on the spot—a fact that will earn a lot of trust and respect.

2. *Don't talk too much.* Never talk over other people or take up too much discussion time. Give everyone equal opportunity to speak. In a political debate, candidate performance is often measured at least in part by how many minutes he or she spoke. The opposite holds true in a conversation requiring compromise. The fewer words, the better.

3. *Always take input seriously.* No matter how you feel about someone else's statement, do not discount or ridicule it. It's virtually impossible to walk a remark back once a person feels insulted.

4. *Keep tabs on what has been said.* Whether people agree or disagree with each other's remarks, don't allow any perspectives t o get lost. Make sure the group has responded in some way to everything. When necessary, repeat or summarize statements to keep them fresh and show that you have been paying attention.

5. *Help others speak up.* If a person at the table seems reserved and quiet, consciously ask her what she thinks. She may have a valuable suggestion or had been holding something back. You want everyone to be comfortable about participating and making suggestions.

6. *State your opinion.* While you want to engage in active listening and respectfully acknowledge other speakers, you are also entitled to state your personal opinion when you have the floor. You are allowed to be candid and disagree, as long you maintain professional body language, keep your emotions in check, and don't attack others (including through sarcasm). You should never agree with something when you don't. You may decide to concede the point as part of your compromise, but you must hold true to your beliefs.

7. *Stay concrete and factual, avoiding generalizations.* You will lose the interest and support of the room if you exaggerate, go off on a tangent, or start telling unrelated stories. Stick to the facts.

Above all, be tactful, honest, and diplomatic at all times. The more calm, cool, composed, and professional you are, the more the other party will want to work with you, be receptive to your ideas, and entertain compromise.

We Can Work It Out—With a Little Help from an Objective Party

Sometimes an objective moderator or mediator can help two parties arrive at necessary compromise before things have a chance to become heated. Both sides of the discussion must mutually agree to this individual in advance of the meeting; there shouldn't be any surprises.

There are distinctions between a moderator and mediator, of course. A good moderator will keep the discussion moving, enable all points to be properly aired, and ensure everyone makes a contribution. A strong mediator will not only manage the conversation, but will also help the parties find common ground and places where equivalent compromises can be made.

The Moral Imperative

In a fascinating paper entitled "Possible Ways to Promote Compromise," Brian Tomasik presents an intellectual treatise on ways to join people together with different belief systems through the art of compromise. Essentially, we all hold different moral views associated with our group associations that prevent us from being able to relate to and accept beliefs that fall outside our frame of reference. In a specific religion, for example, symbols and rituals can be as powerful as an "electrical current" to unite and charge a group of people with shared views. I'm not being sarcastic when I say that this type of group power exists in politics and even in sports fandom, where symbols (team colors, logos, and even mascots) represent the collective.

If everything is handled correctly according to all of the suggestions in this chapter, yet the parties still fail to connect and compromise, is the deal kaput? How can two diametrically opposed philosophies overcome "us vs. them" thinking and ever hope to find a compromise?

The answer is an emphatic "yes." Let's consider a sports analogy. Fan support for a major league baseball team can occasionally get pretty fierce, go overboard, and maybe even lead to a physical brawl under the right circumstances (especially when alcohol is involved). Do you think New

York Yankees fans and Boston Red Sox fans will ever join a group hug and compromise their team loyalty? Highly unlikely. But they do share *at least* one major thing in common: *the love of baseball.*

When it comes to improving our QOZs, we all have a distinct commonality: *pride in our country.* Liberals and Conservatives may hash it out on many issues and never budge an inch either way, but both sides can see eye-to-eye on one thing: *the love of the United States of America.* A Conservative Republican may see QOZ legislation as a way for Americans to build significant wealth through capital gains savings, which they believe will ultimately funnel back into boosting the economy. A Liberal Democrat may see QOZs as a way for socio-economically struggling people to obtain better housing and higher paying employment that otherwise would never happen.

I propose that we choose to say that neither perspective is right or wrong. I'd like to close this final chapter by offering an important, if controversial suggestion. Let's mutually agree to compromise by putting some blinders on about the *why* in order to consider the *what if?* Call this common denominator what you will—the love of country or patriotism—the benefit of the QOZ initiative will work if we become oblivious to party lines and focus on the end result:

What if...we were to work together to create a better, stronger America for all Americans?

A FINAL CALL TO ACTION

Now that you've had the opportunity to learn all there is to know about QOFs and QOZs, I hope you share my passion for this important endeavor and have incorporated it into your own life's purpose. Assuming that's the case, there is only one thing left for you to do: *Help spread the message!*

I would like this book to serve as a manifesto—a call to action—to maximize QOF investments in QOZs and make our urban and rural communities better, which strengthens our nation as a whole. This national initiative is accelerating at a frantic pace as communities are starting to catch on and learn about all of the good that QOZs can accomplish. Since I began work on this book, areas as far-flung as Washington D.C., Atlanta, GA, and Dallas, TX have begun to initiate a wide-range of exciting projects that have the potential to transform and revitalize their communities.

I am confident that what we are seeing now is just a tiny glimpse of what is possible. Once one community starts embarking on projects, others will follow suit...and another...and another...and so forth.

We can work together to make this effort truly colossal by sharing our QOZ success stories: how specific neighborhoods are improving and lives are being changed. I want to see people exchange best practices and methods so one community can help another. I would love to discover all of the "next big things" being developed in QOZs—not only to cheer folks on and lend my voice and support, but potentially for my own personal investments. I don't want to miss out on an exciting opportunity, either!

Thank you kindly for joining me on this wonderful and exciting journey. As you venture off on your own, I leave you with a pearl of wisdom from legendary basketball coach John Wooden: "Be true to yourself. Make each day a masterpiece. Help others. Drink deeply from good books. Make friendship a fine art. Build a shelter against a rainy day."

SOURCES

In addition to the sources cited below, much of the content is based on the Circle of Success Business Management Process, created by the author, Jim White. For more information, please contact JL White International, LLC at jlwhiteinternational.com.

He is also the author of numerous works, including:

- *What's My Purpose, A Journey of Professional Growth,* ebook and paperback, JL White International, LLC, 2007.

- *Manage Your Stress and Live Your Life,* paperback, JL White International, LLC, 2016.

- *Leadership and Influence: Inspiring Motivation in People,* paperback, JL White International, LLC, paperback, 2018.

Chapter One:

Florida, Richard. "How the 1% is Pulling America's Cities and Regions Apart," CityLab.com, April 3, 2019. https://www.citylab.com/ equity/ 2019/04/economic-inequality-geographic-divide-map-census-income- data/586222/

No Author. "Projected GDP Ranking 2019-2023." http://statisticstimes. com/ economy/projected-world-gdp-ranking.php

Ingraham, Christopher. "The Richest 1 Percent Now Owns More of the Country's Wealth Than at Any time in the Past 50 Years," *The Washington Post,* December 6, 2017. https://www.washingtonpost.com/ news/wonk/wp/2017/12/06/the-richest-1-percent-now-owns-more-of-the-countrys-wealth-than-at-any-time-in-the-past-50-years/?utm_ term=.d3ebe090f02f

Economic Innovation Group. "From Great Recession to Great Reshuffling: Charting a Decade of Change Across American Communities: Findings from the 2018 Distressed Communities Index," October 2018. https://eig.org/wp-content/uploads/2018/10/2018-dci.pdf

Holder, Sarah. "America's Most and Least Distressed Cities." CityLab, September 17, 2017. https://www.citylab.com/equity/2017/09/distressed-communities/ 541044/

No Author. https://www.gilbertedi.com/why-gilbert/

Blodgett, Tom. "Gilbert Looks to Become 'City of the Future,' Ward Off Decline That Troubles Many U.S. Municipalities," CommunityImpact.com, February 27, 2019. https://communityimpact.com/phoenix/gilbert/development-construction/2019/02/27/town-looks-to-ward-off-decline-that-troubles-many-municipalities-in-u-s/

Goff, Jenna. "Fast Facts About Philadelphia," PBS.org, July 22, 2016. https://www.pbs.org/weta/washingtonweek/blog-post/fast-facts-about-philadelphia

Stebbins, Samuel and Comen, Evan. "50 Worst Cities to Live In," 247WallSt.com, June 10, 2018. https://247wallst.com/special-report/ 2018/06/10/50-worst-cities-to-live-in-3/4/

Eltagouri, Marwa and Wong, Grace. "Chicago Area Leads U.S. in Population Loss, Sees Drop for 2nd Year in a Row," *The Chicago Tribune*, March 23, 2017. https://www.chicagotribune.com/news/local/breaking/ct-chicago-census-population-loss-met-20170322-story.html

Greenhut, Steven. "Formerly Bankrupt Stockton Is Fiscally Healthy Again, But Offers Warning to Others," June 28, 2018. https://californiapolicy center.org/formerly-bankrupt-stockton-is-fiscally-healthy-again-but-offers-warning-to-others/

Economic Innovation Group. "2018 Distressed Communities Index." https://eig.org/dci

Thompson, Cadie and Matousek, Mark. "America's Infrastructure Is Decaying—Here's a Look at How Terrible Things Have Gotten," *Business Insider,* February 5, 2019. https://www.businessinsider .com/ asce-gives-us-infrastructure-a-d-2017-3

Graham, David. A. "How Did the Oroville Dam Crisis Get So Dire?," *The Atlantic*, February 13, 2017. https://www.theatlantic.com/ national/ archive/2017/02/how-did-the-oroville-dam-get-so-bad/516429/

Greenhut, Steven. "City Finance Director Says Oroville Faces Specter of Bankruptcy," rstreet.com, September 28, 2017. https://www. rstreet.org/2017/09/28/city-finance-director-says-oroville-faces-specter-of-bankruptcy/

Tabuchi, Hiroko. "300 Billion War Beneath the Street: Fighting to Replace America's Water Pipes," *The New York Times*, November 10, 2017. https:// www.nytimes.com/2017/11/10/climate/water-pipes-plastic-lead.html

Rivera, Ramon. "Aging Water Infrastructure Threatens Drinking Water Quality," Diamond Scientific, October 8, 2018. https://diamondsci. com/blog/aging-water-infrastructure-causes-water-quality-issues/

No Author. https://ycharts.com/indicators/detroit_mi_unemployment_ rate

No Author. https://tradingeconomics.com/united-states/ unemployment-rate

Beyer, Scott. "Why Has Detroit Continued To Decline?," *Forbes*, July 31, 2018. https://www.forbes.com/sites/scottbeyer/2018/07/31/ why-has-detroit-continued-to-decline/#70f294303fbe

Stateside Staff and Horan, Joey. "Detroit's Controversial Drainage Fee and Michigan's Struggles to Fund Stormwater Infrastructure," Michigan Radio, February 18, 2019. https://www.michiganradio. org/post/detroit-s-controversial-drainage-fee-and-michigan-s-struggles-fund-stormwater-infrastructure

Bentle, Kyle; Berlin, Jonathon; Mahr, Joe; and Yoder, Chad. "Are Bridges Near You Deteriorating?," *Chicago Tribune*, February 6, 2019. https://www.chicagotribune.com/news/ct-met-viz-chicago-area-bridges-in-need-of-repair-htmlstory.html

No Author. "25 of the Most Dangerous Cities in America." https://www.usatoday.com/picture-gallery/travel/experience/america/2018/10/17/25-most-dangerous-cities-america/1669467002/

No Author. https://www.drugabuse.gov/drugs-abuse/opioids/opioid-overdose-crisis#ten

No Author. https://health.baltimorecity.gov/opioid-overdose/baltimore-city-overdose-prevention-and-response-information

Lopez, German. "The Opioid Epidemic Is Increasingly Killing Black Americans. Baltimore Is Ground Zero," Vox.com, April 1, 2019. https://www.vox.com/policy-and-politics/2019/3/22/18262179/baltimore-opioid-epidemic-overdose-addiction-treatment

Elliott, Megan. "American Companies Keep Sending Thousands of Jobs Overseas," CheatSheet.com, January 12, 2018 https://www.cheatsheet.com/money-career/american-companies-sent-jobs-overseas.html/

Shephard, Alex. "Amazon Scammed America's Hurting Cities," *The New Republic*, November 12, 2018.

Chapter Two:
No Author. https://www.census.gov

No Author. https://www.internetworldstats.com/stats8.htm

Donnelly, Grace. "Here's Why Life Expectancy in the U.S. Dropped Again This Year," *Fortune*, February 9, 2018. http://fortune. com/2018/02/09/us-life-expectancy-dropped-again/

No Author. "Heart Disease and Stroke Statistics-2019 At-a-Glance," American Heart Association, 2019. https://healthmetrics.heart. org/wp-content/uploads/2019/02/At-A-Glance-Heart-Disease-and-Stroke-Statistics–2019.pdf

No Author. https://tradingeconomics.com/united-states/ unemployment-rate

Economic Innovation Group. "From Great Recession to Great Reshuffling: Charting a Decade of Change Across American Communities: Findings from the 2018 Distressed Communities Index," October 2018. https://eig.org/wp-content/uploads/2018/10/2018-dci.pdf

No Author. "These Are the 50 Best Places in America for Starting a Business," *Inc. Magazine,* Undated. https://www.inc.com/surge-cities/best-places-start-business.html

Chapter Three:
No Author. https://www.govtrack.us/congress/votes/115-2017/s303

Kaplan, Thomas and Rappeport, Alan. "Republican Tax Bill Passes Senate in 51-48 Vote," *The New York Times*, December 19, 2017. https://www.nytimes.com/2017/12/19/us/politics/tax-bill-vote-congress.html

Krugman, Paul. "The Biggest Tax Scam in History," *The New York Times*, November 27, 2017. https://www.nytimes.com/2017/11/27/ opinion/senate-tax-bill-scam.html

Chol, David. "'Irresponsible, Reckless, Unjust, and Just Plain Cruel': Democrats Blast GOP Tax Bill After It Passes," *Business Insider*, December 20, 2017. https://www.businessinsider.com/republican-tax-bill-democrats-respond-2017-12

No Author. https://www.booker.senate.gov/?p=press_release&id=713

Clifford, Catherine. "Billionaire Warren Buffett: 'I Don't Need a Tax Cut' in a Society with So Much Inequality," CNBC.com, October 4, 2017. https://www.cnbc.com/2017/10/04/billionaire-warren-buffett-i-dont-need-a-tax-cut.html

Tankersley, Jim. "Tucked into the Tax Bill, a Plan to Help Distressed America," *The New York Times*, January 28, 2018.https://www.nytimes.com/2018/01/29/business/tax-bill-economic-recovery-opportunity-zones.html

Bernstein, Jared, Center on Budget and Policy Priorities; and Hassett, Kevin A., American Enterprise Institute. Economic Innovation Group, April, 2015. https://eig.org/wp-content/uploads/2015/04/Unlocking-Private-Capital-to-Facilitate-Growth.pdf

Chapter Four:
No Author. https://libguides.lib.msu.edu/tracts

No Author. "5 Open Questions on Qualified Opportunity Zones." https://wealth.northerntrust.com/articles/five-open-questions-on-qualified-opportunity-zones/

Barton, Tom. "Here's What Mike Pence had to say about Tim Scott, SC's Opportunity Zone Project," TheState.com, February 21, 2019. https://www.thestate.com/news/politicsgovernment/article226532115.html#storylink=cpy

Chapter Five:
Chen, James. "What Is a Triple Net Lease (NNN)? Investopedia.com., August 28, 2019. https://www.investopedia.com/terms/t/triple-net-lease-nnn.asp

Chapter Six:
No Author. https://www.brainyquote.com/authors/cory_booker

No Author. http://www.ohiohistorycentral.org/w/Youngstown,_Ohio

No Author. https://www.officialdata.org/1797-dollars-in2017?amount=16000

Posey, Sean. "America's Fastest Shrinking City: The Story of Youngstown, Ohio," The Hampton Institute, June 17, 2013.

Sauter, Michael B.; Stebbins, Samuel; and Comen, Evan. "50 Worst American Cities to Live In," 247wallst.com, June 16, 2017. https://247wallst.com/special-report/2017/06/16/50-worst-cities-to-live-in/7/

No Author. https://www.neighborhoodscout.com/oh/youngstown/crime

No Author. "What's It Like to Live in Youngstown, OH?" https://realestate.usnews.com/places/ohio/youngstown

No Author. http://www.regionalchamber.com/initiativesprograms/opportunityzones

No Author. https://www.philanthropyroundtable.org/almanac/people/philanthropic-quotes

Dennis, Chelsea and Dubb, Steve. "Billionaires Target 'Opportunity Zones'—But Whose Opportunity Are They," *Nonprofit Quarterly*, October 23, 2018. https://nonprofitquarterly.org/billionaires-target-opportunity-zones-but-whose-opportunity-are-they/

No Author. https://www.rockefellerfoundation.org/about-us/news-media/rockefeller-foundation-launches-opportunity-zone-community-capacity-building-initiative-newark-first-city-selected/

Munnelly, Kristen and Dubb, Steve. "Opportunity Zones: Can Philanthropy Provide Accountability When the Law Does Not?" *Nonprofit Quarterly*, May 29, 2019. https://nonprofitquarterly.org/opportunity-zones-can-philanthropy-provide-accountability-when-the-law-does-not/

No Author. https://kresge.org/who-we-are

No Author. "Kresge Foundation Commits $22M to Back Arctaris, Community Capital Management Opportunity Zone Funds." https://kresge.org/news/kresge-foundation-commits-22m-back-arctaris-community-capital-management-opportunity-zone-funds

Evans, Cody and Dasewicz, Agnes. "How Foundations Can Help Opportunity Zone Communities Succeed," Stanford Social Innovation Review, February 7, 2019. https://ssir.org/articles/entry/how_foundations_can_help_opportunity_zone_communities_succeed#

Bailey, John. "The Education Opportunity in Opportunity Zones," EducationNext.com, July 2, 2019. https://www.educationnext.org/education-opportunity-zones-incentivized-investment-distressed-communites-close-prosperity-gap/

No Author. http://www.21csf.org/csf-home/aboutus.asp

No Author. https://www.brainyquote.com/quotes/henry_adams_108018

Calfas, Jennifer. "This Map Shows the Average Teacher Salary in Every State," Money.com, May 23, 2018. http://money.com/money/5287489/average-teacher-salary-by-state/

Stoltzfus, Kate. "From Teacher Villages to Tiny Homes: Housing Benefits for Educators," Education Week, January 23, 2018. https://www.edweek.org/ew/articles/2018/01/24/from-teacher-villages-to-tiny-homes-housing.html

Brune Adrian. "He Built a $150 Million Village...for Schoolteachers," Ozy.com May 14, 2018. https://www.ozy.com/rising-stars/he-built-a-150-million-village-for-schoolteachers/86028

Isaacson, Greg. "Starwood Capital to Launch 1st Opportunity Zone Project," CommercialPropertyExecutive.com, May 10, 2019. https://www.cpexecutive.com/post/starwood-capital-jumps-into-bronx-qoz-with-charter-school-project/

Cohen, Rachel M. "The Tax Break That Could Fund New Charter Schools," CityLab.com, April 23, 2019.

No Author. https://www.collegebasics.com/going-to-college/benefits-of-campus-living/

Childs, Mary. "What One of the First Qualified Opportunity Funds Is Doing," *Barron's*, April 9, 2019. https://www.barrons.com/articles/what-one-of-the-first-qualified-opportunity-funds-is-doing-51554816569

No Author. https://www.bestcolleges.com/features/top-30-historically-black-colleges/

No Author. "EDA Focuses on Qualified Opportunity Zones," April 19, 2019. https://www.eda.gov/news/blogs/2019/04/19/opportunity-zones.htm

No Author. https://globalresilience.northeastern.edu/category/oppzone/

No Author. https://www.ojjdp.gov/grants/solicitations/FY2019/Gang Support.pdf

Policymap Team. "Health Care and Opportunity Zones: The Game Begins," April 1, 2019. https://www.policymap.com/2019/04/health-care-and-opportunity

Chapter Seven:

Wolf, Renita. *Investment Ready*, publisher TBD.
No Author. https://opportunity-funds.com/fortune-favors-the-prepared/

Brickey, Bill; Shea, Carey; and Watkins, Alisha. "My Community Has an Opportunity Zone—Now What?" PlanteMoran.com, February 22, 2019. https://www.plantemoran.com/explore-our-thinking/insight/2019/02/my-community-has-an-opportunity-zone-now-what

Chapter Eight:

Augur, Hannah. "Accelerator and Incubator Alternatives," *Forbes*, December 25, 2015.b https://www.forbes.com/sites/forbes realestatecouncil/2018/06/28/now-is-the-time-to-invest-in-distressed-communities-across-america/#d0e0ed53ae41

No Author. https://www.u-s-history.com/pages/h2119.html

Bunn, Rachel. "Here Are Some of PA's 'Most Distressed' Communities," *PennLive Patriot News*, Undated. https://www.pennlive.com/news/2016/03/why_are_these_communities_penn.html

Economic Innovation Group. "EIG Webinar on Erie, PA: A City Comes Together to Unlock its Potential." https://eig.org/news/eig-webinar-on-erie-pa

Carlson, Debbie. "9 Sectors That Investors Should Watch in 2019," *U.S. News*, December 28, 2018. https://money.usnews.com/investing/stock-market-news/slideshows/9-sectors-that-investors-should-watch-in-2019

No Author. https://www.entrepreneur.com/encyclopedia/business-incubator

Katz, Bruce. "Who Will Lead the Change?" *The Philadelphia Citizen*, August 26, 2019. https://thephiladelphiacitizen.org/philly-opportunity-zones/

Margulies, Joseph. "Communities Need Neighborhood Trusts," Stanford Social Innovation Review, Spring 2019. https://ssir.org/articles/entry/communities_need_neighborhood_trusts

D'Angelo, Matt and Staff. "How Accelerators, Incubators and Startup Collectives Drive Growth," *Business News Daily*, October 31, 2018. https://www.businessnewsdaily.com/11119-accelerator-startup-incubator-growth.html

No Author. https://www.accenture.com/us-en/about/innovation-centers-index

Chapter Nine:
No Author. https://www.mystockoptions.com/content/what-is-the-difference-between-a-merger-an-acquisition-a-divestiture-and-a-spinoff

No Author. http://taxgrouppartners.com/tax-alerts/2018-12/opportunity-zones.php

Szmigiera, M. "Mergers and Acquisitions – Statistics and Facts," Statista.com, October 10, 2019. https://www.statista.com/topics/1146/mergers-and-acquisitions/

No Author. https://www.investopedia.com/articles/investing/111014/top-reasons-why-ma-deals-fail.asp

No Author. "Fools Rush In: 37 Of The Worst Corporate M&A Flops," CBInsights.com, October 30, 2018. https://www.cbinsights.com/research/merger-acquisition-corporate-fails/

Seth, Shobhit. "Top Reasons Why M&A Deals Fail," Investopedia.com, May 21, 2019. https://www.investopedia.com/articles/investing/111014/top-reasons-why-ma-deals-fail.asp

Nasiripour, Shahien. "Which Industries Lost/Gained Jobs In The Great Recession?," *The Huffington Post*, December 6, 2017. https://www.huffpost.com/entry/which-industries-lostgain_n_525504

Fontinelle, Eric. "Buffett's Biggest Mistakes," Investopedia.com, June 25, 2019. https://www.investopedia.com/financial-edge/0210/buffetts-biggest-mistakes.aspx

No Author. "Opportunity Zones Aren't Just for Real Estate," *Crains New York*, May 24, 2019. https://www.crainsnewyork.com/sponsored-opportunity-zones/opportunity-zones-arent-just-real-estate

Goedhart, Marc; Koller, Tim; and Wessels, David. "The Six Types of Successful Acquisitions," McKinsey.com, May 2017. https://www.mckinsey.com/business-functions/strategy-and-corporate-finance/our-insights/the-six-types-of-successful-acquisitions

Porter, John. "Virgin Galactic to Become the First Space Tourism Company to Go Public," theverge.com, July 9, 2019. https://www.theverge.com/2019/7/9/20687323/virgin-galactic-publicly-traded-richard-branson-space-tourism-profitability

No Author. https://www.businessroundtable.org/about-us

Chapter Ten:
Post, Jennifer. "What Is a PEST Analysis?," Business News Daily, September 21, 2018. https://www.businessnewsdaily.com/5512-pest-analysis-definition-examples-templates.html

No Author. "Considering 'Purpose': What the Top Corporate Law Judge Says," Directors&Boards, Undated. http://editor.ne16.com/vo/?FileID=b76b9c7a-ea3f-4388-b368-c1a66378429c&m=09735dff-7fde-41a8-9fca-18a01bc6a46a&MailID=1578129&listid=1002910&RecipientID=4437701618

Chapter Thirteen:
Lee, Aaron. "30 Legendary Startup Pitch Decks And What You Can Learn From Them," Piktochart.com, Undated. https://piktochart.com/blog/startup-pitch-decks-what-you-can-learn/

No Author. https://www.google.com/search/howsearchworks/mission/

No Author. https://www.lowes.com/l/company-information.html

No Author. https://newscenter.dollargeneral.com/company-facts/fastfacts/

Riley, Patrick. "This is How to Build Trust with Your Investors Beyond Your Actual Pitch," gan.co., February 26, 2019. https://www.gan.co/blog/investor-trust-beyond-your-pitch/

Chapter Fourteen:

No Author. https://www.ranker.com/list/famous-american-inventors-list/reference

Kelly, Martin. "Notable American Inventors of the Industrial Revolution," Thoughtco.com, July 18, 2019. https://www.thoughtco.com/top-significant-industrial-revolution-inventors-104725

No Author. http://www.american-inventor.com/great-inventors.aspx

[No last name], Katherine. "Sisters in Innovation 20 Women Inventors You Should Know," AMightyGirl.com, September 19, 2018. https://www.amightygirl.com/blog?p=12223

Hetherington, Toni. Five of the World's Biggest Ideas Started with Inventors Working out of Garages," Kidsnews.com, April 8, 2018. https://www.kidsnews.com.au/technology/five-of-the-worlds-biggest-ideas-started-with-inventors-working-out-of-garages/news-story/f712d61ce069c53610d0e1afe027b978

Horowitz, Julia; Pham, Sharise; and CNN Business. "Hyundai Is Investing $35 Billion in Autonomous Driving and Electric Cars," CNN Business, October 15, 2019. https://www.cnn.com/2019/10/15/business/hyundai-invest-tech/index.html

Smale, Thomas. "7 Tech Trends to Watch Out for In 2020," Entrepreneur.com, September 2, 2019. https://www.entrepreneur.com/article/338514

No Author. "Our Picks for the Top 10 Coolest Sustainable Inventions," 1millionwomen.com.au. https://www.1millionwomen.com.au/blog/our-picks-top-10-coolest-sustainable-inventions/

Dillow, Clay. "12 Reasons 2020 Will Be an Awesome Year," NBC News, undated. http://www.nbcnews.com/id/43015182/ns/technology_and_science-innovation/t/reasons-will-be-awesome-year/#.XadalC2ZOWg

Patton, Wendy and Leonard, Michael. "Assessing Opportunity Zones in Ohio," PolicyMattersOhio.com, September 19, 2018. https://www.policymattersohio.org/research-policy/quality-ohio/revenue-budget/tax-policy/assessing-opportunity-zones-in-ohio

Chapter Sixteen:
No Author. https://www.brainyquote.com/topics/compromise-quotes

Fisher, Roger and Ury, William. *Getting to Yes: Revised and Updated*, Penguin, 2011.

Tomaski, Brian. "Possible Ways to Promote Compromise," Foundational Research Institute, updated February 5, 2016. https://foundational-research.org/possible-ways-to-promote-compromise/

Conclusion:
Abello, Oscar Perry. "Which Past Will Be Prologue for Opportunity Zones in Atlanta?," NextCity.org, September 26, 2019. https://nextcity.org/daily/entry/which-past-will-be-prologue-for-opportunity-zones-in-atlanta

Simek, Peter. "Developers Look to Opportunity Zones to Reshape Dallas," dmagazine.com, 2019. https://www.dmagazine.com/publications/d-ceo/2019/october/dallas-opportunity-zones-fair-park-cedars/

No Author. https://www.brainyquote.com/quotes/john_wooden_446989

GLOSSARY

Accelerator: an organization usually lasting between three-to-six months that removes roadblocks that are bogging down the growth or success of a new business.

ACE: acronym for Accuracy, Clarity, and Emphasis with regard to business objectives.

Acquisition: any time one company purchases another—whether it is merged with the acquiring company or not.

Adaptability: having the ability to rapidly change processes to meet new environmental variables, which may include innovation and challenges.

Asset: any entity owned by the *Qualified Opportunity Zone Business (QOZB)*, such as stock, real estate, equipment, etc., which may be eligible for capital gains savings upon its sale.

Asset Test: one of the special rules that must be applied in a *Qualified Opportunity Zone Business (QOZB)* in order for an investor to receive capital gains tax savings.

Business Map: a visual depiction of the system of relationships and processes within and around organizations.

Business Model: the elevator pitch for what makes a business unique.

Capital Gains: the profit that results from a sale of a capital asset, such as stock, bond, or real estate.

Capital Gains Tax: the amount that may be taxed from the profit on the sale of a capital asset.

Census: document containing a wide range of information gathered and disseminated about an area's population, starting with the number of residents. In the United States, the census is created and maintained by the U.S. Census Bureau.

Compromise (author's definition): an ability to listen to two sides in a disagreement or dispute, concede points on both sides, and arrive at an amicable agreement that satisfies both parties in order to achieve a common goal.

Distressed Community: a rural or urban area that has fallen into a state of severe socio-economic decline.

Divestiture: when a piece (or sections) of a company is separated from the whole and bought by another entity.

EBITDA: an acronym for earnings before interest, tax, depreciation, and amortization. This represents one of the major forms of measuring company performance.

Flywheel: a mechanical object that is used to increase a machine's momentum. The word is used in business to refer to a key aspect of a company that drives its success.

GDP (Gross Domestic Product): a country's measure of economic activity.

Incubator: an organization designed to nurture and develop a new business. The incubator may provide workspace, tools, and other necessities for the business to become a startup.

Infrastructure: the supportive facilities necessary to keep a community running smoothly and safely. This may include water, electricity, roads, bridges, park maintenance, etc.

Innovation Center: a place where new business ideas can be fostered, produced, and tested.

Kaizen: a philosophy of continuous improvement in an organization.

Key Performance Indicators (KPIs): the main performance areas for your specific business.

Lean: in a business context, this refers to achieving the shortest possible cycle time through the tireless reduction of waste.

Low-income Community: a *population census tract* that has a poverty level of at least 20%. Alternatively: it may be considered "low-income" if the area is not located within a metropolitan area and the median income for the area does not exceed 80% of the statewide median income; or, in the case of a tract located within a metropolitan area, the median family income for the area does not exceed 80% of the greater of the statewide family income or the metropolitan area median family income.

M&A: See separate *Merger* and *Acquisition* entries.

Maker/Hackerspace: entity that provides resources that might be too expensive for a startup.

Meetup Platform: a place where people get together and force idea creation or production in a brief period of time. Also sometimes known as a "Hackathon."

Merger: when one company is bought by another and then folded into that organization or into one of its subsidiaries to form a unified legal entity.

Opportunity Fund: See *Qualified Opportunity Fund (QOF)*.

Opportunity Zone: See *Qualified Opportunity Zone (QOZ)*.

Opportunity Zone Business: See *Qualified Opportunity Zone Business (QOZB)*.

Original use: one of the special rules that must be applied in order for an investor to receive capital gains tax savings on a *Qualified Opportunity Zone Business Property (QOZBP)*.

Pareto Principle, the: named after Italian economist Vilfredo Paredo, when applied in business, this philosophy directs companies to "Concentrate on the vital few; ignore the trivial many." In other words, 80% of a problem is often caused by 20% of the contributing factors.

PEST Analysis: an assessment of the impact of outside forces on your business. The acronym stands for **P**olitical factors, **E**conomic factors, **So**cial factors; and **T**echnological factors.

Population Census Tract: a neighborhood identified by the U.S. Census Bureau for analyzing the resident populations. Typically, a population census tract consists of 2,500-8,000 people. See also *Qualified Census Tract (QCT)*.

Post-Mortem: a group review of a completed process or project to determine what went right (in order to repeat this) and/or what went wrong (in order to find root cause and prevent future occurrence).

Purpose: An individual or company's "reason for being." Sometimes a brief written statement, one's personal *purpose* explains how his or her life is "being lived." A company *purpose* conveys the underlying meaning behind why the company exists and often helps unite employees with a common philosophical message.

QCT: See *Qualified Census Tract (QCT)*.

QOF: See *Qualified Opportunity Fund (QOF)*.

QOZ: See *Qualified Opportunity Zone (QOZ)*.

QOZB: See *Qualified Opportunity Zone Business (QOZB)*.

QOZBP: See *Qualified Opportunity Zone Business Property (QOZBP)*.

QOZP: See *Qualified Opportunity Zone Property (QOZP)*.

QOZPI: See *Qualified Opportunity Zone Partnership Interest (QOZPI)*.

QOZS: See *Qualified Opportunity Zone Stock (QOZS)*.

Qualified Census Tract (QCT): any census tract (or equivalent geographic area defined by the Census Bureau) in which at least 50% of households have an income less than 60% of the Area Median Gross Income (AMGI). See also *Population Census Tract*.

Qualified Opportunity Fund (QOF): an investment vehicle created as part of the *Tax Cuts and Jobs Act (TCJA) of 2017* enacted in December 2017 to incentivize investment in *Qualified Opportunity Zones (QOZs)*—approved distressed areas.

Qualified Opportunity Zone (QOZ): a distressed, low-income area that has been approved by the definitions provided in Subchapter Z of the TCJA. An investor may invest his or her capital gains in the *Qualified Opportunity Fund (QOF)* in this area to benefit from capital gains tax savings.

Qualified Opportunity Zone Business (QOZB): a business entity that has been approved within a *Qualified Opportunity Zone (QOZ)* and is investor- funded with *Qualified Opportunity Funds (QOFs)*.

Qualified Opportunity Zone Business Property (QOZBP): any tangible property—such as real estate and equipment—that has been purchased after December 31, 2017 and is situated within the approved *Qualified Opportunity Zone (QOZ)* area. This real estate, equipment, etc. must be used exclusively for QOZ purposes and be substantially improved after the purchase.

Qualified Opportunity Zone Partnership Interest (QOZPI): refers to any equity interest in a partnership if such interest was acquired by a QOF after December 31, 2017 solely in exchange for cash. At the time such interest was acquired, the QOZPI had to be a *QOZ Business (QOZB)* used specifically for purposes directly associated with the approved area.

Qualified Opportunity Zone Property (QOZP): any type of property that falls into one of the following definitions: *Qualified Opportunity Zone Stock (QOZS), Qualified Opportunity Zone Partnership Interest (QOZPI),* or *Qualified Opportunity Zone Business Property (QOZBP)*. QOZBP must meet four criteria: (1) It must be used in the trade or business of a QOF. (2) It must be acquired by purchase after December 31, 2017. (3) It must either be originally used by the QOF in the QOZ or substantially improved by the QOF. (4) During substantially all of the time it is held by the QOF or the QOZB.

Qualified Opportunity Zone Stock (QOZS): any stock in a domestic corporation, as long as it was acquired after December 31, 2017 at its original issue—directly or through an underwriter—from the corporation solely in exchange for cash. The corporation must specifically be an existing or new *QOZ Business (QOZB)* used solely for purposes directly associated with the approved area.

Recession: a severe economic drop in economic activity, often resulting from decreased spending.

Six Sigma: a method of measuring quality and performance in an organization.

SMART Goals: a strategy often implemented by human resource professionals with regard to annual employee performance. The acronym stands for: **S**pecific, **M**easurable, **A**ttainable, **R**elevant, and **T**imely.

Spinoff: when a *divested* part of a company becomes a brand new separate company that is not assimilated into the corporate hierarchy of the parent company.

Startup Residence: a city-funded support initiative that helps improve a respective community, often combatting civic challenges.

Streamlining: general term for a process that meets its intended result in the fewest number of steps.

Subchapter Z: See *Tax Cuts and Jobs Act (TCJA) of 2017.*

Substantially Improved Test: one of the special rules that must be applied in a *Qualified Opportunity Zone Business Property (QOZBP)* in order for an investor to receive capital gains tax savings. The *Qualified Opportunity Fund (QOF)* investment amount must double the value of the property itself.

SWOT Analysis: assessment of a company's **S**trengths, **W**eaknesses, **O**pportunities, and **T**hreats.

Tax Cuts and Jobs Act (TCJA) of 2017: The most exhaustive tax law legislation approved since the Internal Revenue Code of 1986. Signed by President Donald J. Trump on December 22, 2017, support for the TCJA was divided among party lines. The TCJA includes Subchapter Z, which outlines rules for *Qualified Opportunity Zones (QOZs)* and *Qualified Opportunity Funds (QOFs)* that enable investors to have capital gains savings while investing in approved distressed communities.

TCJA: See *Tax Cuts and Jobs Act (TCJA) of 2017.*

Teacher Village: an area of a community devoted to affordable teacher housing.

Triple Net (NNN) Lease: one in which the tenant is completely responsible for all costs, including the rent; taxes; building insurance; and maintenance fees.

Unique Selling Proposition (USP): The attributes that make a company stand out makes it stand out against the competition.

USP: See *Unique Selling Proposition (USP).*

Values (author's definition): Tell the truth. Do what you say. Lead by example. Conduct your business with integrity. Be accountable.

EXCERPT FROM THE TAX CUTS AND JOBS ACT (TCJA) OF 2017

The following is an excerpt of Subchapter Z culled from the Tax Cuts and Jobs Act (TCJA) of 2017. For access to a PDF of the complete TCJA document, you can find it here: **https://www.congress.gov/115/bills/hr1/BILLS-115hr1enr.pdf**. *For updates to the tax law, go to the IRS website:* **https://www.irs.gov/tax-reform**.

"Subchapter Z—Opportunity Zones

"Sec. 1400Z–1. Designation.

"Sec. 1400Z–2. Special rules for capital gains invested in opportunity zones.

"SEC. 1400Z–1. DESIGNATION.

"(a) QUALIFIED OPPORTUNITY ZONE DEFINED.—For the purposes of this subchapter, the term 'qualified opportunity zone' means a population census tract that is a low-income community that is designated as a qualified opportunity zone.

"(b) DESIGNATION.—

"(1) IN GENERAL.—For purposes of subsection (A), a population census tract that is a low-income community is designated as a qualified opportunity zone if—

"(A) not later than the end of the determination period, the chief executive officer of the State in which the tract is located—

"(i) nominates the tract for designation as a qualified opportunity zone, and

"(ii) notifies the Secretary in writing of such nomination, and

"(B) the Secretary certifies such nomination and designates such tract as a qualified opportunity zone before the end of the consideration period.

"(2) EXTENSION OF PERIODS.—A chief executive officer of a State may request that the Secretary extend either the determination or consideration period, or both (determined without regard to this subparagraph), for an additional 30 days.

"(c) OTHER DEFINITIONS.—For purposes of this subsection—

"(1) LOW-INCOME COMMUNITIES.—The term 'low-income community' has the same meaning as when used in section 45D(e).

"(2) DEFINITION OF PERIODS.— "(A) CONSIDERATION PERIOD.—The term 'consideration period' means the 30-day period beginning on the date on which the Secretary receives notice under subsection (b)(1)(A)(ii), as extended under subsection (b)(2).

"(B) DETERMINATION PERIOD.—The term determination period' means the 90-day period beginning of the enactment of the Tax Cuts and Jobs Act, as extended under subsection (b)(2).

"(3) STATE.—For purposes of this section, the term 'State' includes any possession of the United States.

"(d) NUMBER OF DESIGNATIONS.—

"(1) IN GENERAL.—Except as provided by paragraph (2), the number of population census tracts in a State that may be designated as qualified opportunity zones under this section may not exceed 25 percent of the number of low-income communities in the State.

"(2) EXCEPTION.—If the number of low-income communities in a State is less than 100, then a total of 25 of such tracts may be designated as qualified opportunity zones.

"(e) DESIGNATION OF TRACTS CONTIGUOUS WITH LOW-INCOME COMMUNITIES.—

"(1) IN GENERAL.—A population census tract that is not a low-income community may be designated as a qualified opportunity zone under this section if—

"(A) the tract is contiguous with the low-income community that is designated as a qualified opportunity zone, and

"(B) the median family income of the tract does not exceed 125 percent of the median family income of the low-income community with which the tract is contiguous.

"(2) LIMITATION.—Not more than 5 percent of the population census tracts designated in a State as a qualified opportunity zone may be designated under paragraph (1).

"(f) PERIOD FOR WHICH DESIGNATION IS IN EFFECT.—A designation as a qualified opportunity zone shall remain in effect for the period beginning on the date of the designation and ending at the close of the 10th calendar year beginning on or after such date of designation.

"SEC. 1400Z–2. SPECIAL RULES FOR CAPITAL GAINS INVESTED IN OPPORTUNITY ZONES.

"(a) IN GENERAL.—

"(1) TREATMENT OF GAINS.—In the case of gain from the sale to, or exchange with, an unrelated person of any property held by the taxpayer, at the election of the taxpayer—

"(A) gross income for the taxable year shall not include so much of such gain as does not exceed the aggregate amount invested by the taxpayer in a qualified opportunity fund during the 180-day period beginning on the date of such sale or exchange,

"(B) the amount of gain excluded by subparagraph

(A) shall be included in gross income as provided by subsection (b), and

"(C) subsection (c) shall apply.

"(2) ELECTION.—No election may be made under paragraph

(1)—

"(A) with respect to a sale or exchange if an election previously made with respect to such sale or exchange is in effect, or

"(B) with respect to any sale or exchange after December 31, 2026.

"(b) DEFERRAL OF GAIN INVESTED IN OPPORTUNITY ZONE PROPERTY.—

"(1) YEAR OF INCLUSION.—Gain to which subsection (A)(1)(B) applies shall be included in income in the taxable year which includes the earlier of—

"(A) the date on which such investment is sold or exchanged, or

"(B) December 31, 2026.

"(2) AMOUNT INCLUDIBLE.—

"(A) IN GENERAL.—The amount of gain included in gross income under subsection (A)(1)(A) shall be the excess of—

"(i) the lesser of the amount of gain excluded under paragraph (1) or the fair market value of the investment as determined as of the date described in paragraph (1), over

"(ii) the taxpayer's basis in the investment.

"(B) DETERMINATION OF BASIS.—

"(i) IN GENERAL.—Except as otherwise provided in this clause or subsection (c), the taxpayer's basis in the investment shall be zero.

"(ii) INCREASE FOR GAIN RECOGNIZED UNDER SUBSECTION (A)(1)(B).—The basis in the investment shall be increased by the amount of gain recognized by reason of subsection (A)(1)(B) with respect to such property.

"(iii) INVESTMENTS HELD FOR 5 YEARS.—In the case of any investment held for at least 5 years, the basis of such investment shall be increased by an amount equal to 10 percent of the amount of gain deferred by reason of subsection (A)(1)(A).

"(iv) INVESTMENTS HELD FOR 7 YEARS.—In the case of any investment held by the tax-payer for at least 7 years, in addition to any adjustment made under clause (iii), the basis of such property shall be increased by an amount equal to 5 percent of the amount of gain deferred by reason of subsection (A)(1)(A).

"(c) SPECIAL RULE FOR INVESTMENTS HELD FOR AT LEAST 10 YEARS.—In the case of any investment held by the taxpayer for at least 10 years and with respect to which the taxpayer makes an election under this clause, the basis of such property shall
be equal to the fair market value of such investment on the date that the investment is sold or exchanged.

"(d) QUALIFIED OPPORTUNITY FUND.—For purposes of this section—

"(1) IN GENERAL.—The term 'qualified opportunity fund'
means any investment vehicle which is organized as a corporation or a partnership for the purpose of investing in qualified opportunity zone property (other than another qualified opportunity fund) that holds at least 90 percent of its assets in qualified opportunity zone property, determined by the average of the percentage of qualified opportunity zone property held in the fund as measured—

"(A) on the last day of the first 6-month period of the taxable year of the fund, and

"(B) on the last day of the taxable year of the fund.

"(2) QUALIFIED OPPORTUNITY ZONE PROPERTY.— "(A) IN GENERAL.—The term 'qualified opportunity zone property' means property which is—

"(i) qualified opportunity zone stock,

"(ii) qualified opportunity zone partnership

interest, or

"(iii) qualified opportunity zone business property.

"(B) QUALIFIED OPPORTUNITY ZONE STOCK.—

"(i) IN GENERAL.—Except as provided in clause (ii), the term 'qualified opportunity zone stock' means any stock in a domestic corporation if—

"(I) such stock is acquired by the qualified opportunity fund after December 31, 2017, at its original issue (directly or through an underwriter) from the corporation solely in exchange for cash,

"(II) as of the time such stock was issued, such corporation was a qualified opportunity zone business (or, in the case of a new corporation, such corporation was being organized for purposes of being a qualified opportunity zone business), and

"(III) during substantially all of the qualified opportunity fund's holding period for such stock, such corporation qualified as a qualified opportunity zone business.

"(ii) REDEMPTIONS.—A rule similar to the rule of section 1202(c)(3) shall apply for purposes of this paragraph.

"(C) QUALIFIED OPPORTUNITY ZONE PARTNERSHIP

INTEREST.—The term 'qualified opportunity zone partnership interest' means any capital or profits interest in a domestic partnership if—

"(i) such interest is acquired by the qualified opportunity fund after December 31, 2017, from the partnership solely in exchange for cash,

"(ii) as of the time such interest was acquired, such partnership was a qualified opportunity zone business (or, in the case of a new partnership, such partnership was being organized for purposes of being a qualified opportunity zone business), and

"(iii) during substantially all of the qualified opportunity fund's holding period for such interest, such partnership qualified as a qualified opportunity zone business.

"(D) QUALIFIED OPPORTUNITY ZONE BUSINESS PROPERTY.—

"(i) IN GENERAL.—The term 'qualified opportunity zone business property' means tangible property used in a trade or business of the qualified opportunity

fund if—

"(I) such property was acquired by the qualified opportunity fund by purchase (as defined in section 179(d)(2)) after December 31, 2017,

"(II) the original use of such property in the qualified opportunity zone commences with the qualified opportunity fund or the qualified opportunity fund substantially improves the property, and

"(III) during substantially all of the qualified opportunity fund's holding period for such property, substantially all of the use of such property was in a qualified opportunity zone.

"(ii) SUBSTANTIAL IMPROVEMENT.—For purposes of subparagraph (A)(ii), property shall be treated as substantially improved by the qualified opportunity

fund only if, during any 30-month period beginning after the date of acquisition of such property, additions to basis with respect to such property in the hands of the qualified opportunity fund exceed an amount equal to the adjusted basis of such property at the

beginning of such 30-month period in the hands of the qualified opportunity fund.

"(iii) RELATED PARTY.—For purposes of subparagraph (A)(i), the related person rule of section 179(d)(2) shall be applied pursuant to paragraph (8) of this subsection in lieu of the application of such rule in section 179(d)(2)(A).

"(3) QUALIFIED OPPORTUNITY ZONE BUSINESS.—

"(A) IN GENERAL.—The term 'qualified opportunity zone business' means a trade or business—

"(i) in which substantially all of the tangible property owned or leased by the taxpayer is qualified opportunity zone business property (determined by substituting 'qualified opportunity zone business' for 'qualified opportunity fund' each place it appears in paragraph (2)(D)),

"(ii) which satisfies the requirements of paragraphs (2), (4), and (8) of section 1397C(b), and

"(iii) which is not described in section 144(c)(6)(B).

"(B) SPECIAL RULE.—For purposes of subparagraph (A), tangible property that ceases to be a qualified opportunity zone business property shall continue to be treated as a qualified opportunity zone business property for the lesser of—

"(i) 5 years after the date on which such tangible property ceases to be so qualified, or

"(ii) the date on which such tangible property is no longer held by the qualified opportunity zone business.

"(e) APPLICABLE RULES.—

"(1) TREATMENT OF INVESTMENTS WITH MIXED FUNDS.—In the case of any investment in a qualified opportunity fund only a portion of which consists of investments of gain to which an election under subsection (A) is in effect—

"(A) such investment shall be treated as 2 separate investments, consisting of—

"(i) one investment that only includes amounts to which the election under subsection (A) applies, and

"(ii) a separate investment consisting of other amounts, and

"(B) subsections (A), (b), and (c) shall only apply to the investment described in subparagraph (A)(i).

"(2) RELATED PERSONS.—For purposes of this section, persons are related to each other if such persons are described in section 267(b) or 707(b)(1), determined by substituting '20 percent' for '50 percent' each place it occurs in such sections.

"(3) DECEDENTS.—In the case of a decedent, amounts recognized under this section shall, if not properly includible in the gross income of the decedent, be includible in gross income as provided by section 691.

"(4) REGULATIONS.—The Secretary shall prescribe such regulations as may be necessary or appropriate to carry out the purposes of this section, including—

"(A) rules for the certification of qualified opportunity funds for the purposes of this section,

"(B) rules to ensure a qualified opportunity fund has a reasonable period of time to reinvest the return of capital from investments in qualified opportunity zone stock and qualified opportunity zone partnership interests, and to reinvest proceeds received from the sale or disposition of qualified opportunity zone property, and

"(C) rules to prevent abuse.

"(f) FAILURE OF QUALIFIED OPPORTUNITY FUND TO MAINTAIN INVESTMENT STANDARD.—

"(1) IN GENERAL.—If a qualified opportunity fund fails to meet the 90-percent requirement of subsection (c)(1), the qualified opportunity fund shall pay a penalty for each month it fails to meet the requirement in an amount equal to the product

of—

"(A) the excess of—

"(i) the amount equal to 90 percent of its aggregate assets, over

"(ii) the aggregate amount of qualified opportunity zone property held by the fund, multiplied by

"(B) the underpayment rate established under section 6621(a)(2) for such month.

"(2) SPECIAL RULE FOR PARTNERSHIPS.—In the case that the qualified opportunity fund is a partnership, the penalty imposed by paragraph (1) shall be taken into account proportionately as part of the distributive share of each partner

of the partnership...."

INDEX

interfering, 156
resources, providing, 149
results, focus on, 155
right person for the right job, 154
steps, 154–158
support in disputes, 157
DeMint, Jim, 35
Denver, Colorado, 29
DeSantis, Ron, 80
destiny, 10
Detroit, Michigan, 16, 21, 30, 109
    Water and Sewage Department, 21
developing areas, 184–185
Dexter Shoes, 116
Directors and Boards Forum, 139
disasters, 82
    man-made, 13
    natural, 12, 21
Disney, Roy, 183
Disney, Walt, 183
distress, 12
distressed communities, 12, 14
    business, 18
    cause of, 18–19
    crime, 19, 21–22
    drugs, 19, 21–22
    education, 19
    energy, 19
    health, 19
    infrastructure, 18–21
    minority groups, 18–19
    most distressed list, 16
    people moving away, 13
    population, 40
    public spaces, 19
    recession recovery, 28
    responsibility for with business, 22–24
    safety, 18
    startup businesses, 19
    tourism, 18
    transportation, 19
    water, 19
divestiture, 111–112
dollar, value of, 169
Dollar General, 172
Drexel University, 107
drones, 185
drugs, 19, 21–22, 27, 67, 72

opioid crisis, 21–22
overdoses, 21–22
Dubuque, Iowa, 81
Durant, Oklahoma, 81

early-stage funding deals, 30
EBITDA, 153, 175
economic collapse, 13
    addressing, 176
Economic Development Association
    (EDA), 81, 83
Economic Innovation Group (EIG), 14,
    28, 35–36
Edison, Thomas, 182
education, 53, 72–73, 77–81, 105, 187
    building improvement, 78
    charter schools, 79–80
    colleges and universities, 80–81
    early childhood and after school
        care, 77
    educating government about goals
        of QOZ legislation, 193–194
    elementary and secondary schools,
        77–80
    Historically Black Colleges and
        Universities (HBCU), 80
    message reinforcement, 194
    private meetings with officials and
        community leaders, 193–194
    teacher villages, 78–79
    town halls, 194
Education Next, 77–78
efficiency, 141
ego, 178–179
Einstein, Albert, 182
elevator pitch, 90
elite communities, 14–15
energy, 19, 71, 105, 117, 187
    facilities, 81
    renewable, 15
entertainment centers, 187
entrepreneurship, rate of, 30
environmental, social, and governance
    (ESG) initiatives, 139
Erie, Pennsylvania, 99–100
Erie Downtown Development
    Corporation, 99
Erie Innovation District, 99–100

ABOUT THE AUTHOR: JIM WHITE, PhD

Dr. Jim White is Chairman and CEO of Post Harvest Technologies, Inc. and Growers Ice Company, Inc., Founder and CEO of PHT Opportunity Fund LP, and Founder and President of JL White International, LLC.

Jim is the best-selling author of *What's My Purpose? A Journey of Personal and Professional Growth.* The book, which has been lauded by such industry leaders as Steven M.R. Covey and Jack Canfield, seeks to change readers by helping them to identify key truths while breaking down the main barriers (the Five Masks) to fulfillment.

Jim is also the founder of the customized yearlong leadership and management transformation process, The Circle of Success; Jim White's Classic Movie Series; and The Red Carpet Tour. These innovative events have attracted more than 100,000 participants worldwide, including Fortune 500 CEOs, management teams, entrepreneurs, governments, and trade associations.

Dr. White first found his entrepreneurial spirit at age five when he created his first business—collecting and selling Coke bottles to help support his family. From these humble beginnings, Jim went on to serve his country in Vietnam before entering the corporate world upon his return. Along the way, he would go from high school dropout to academic triumph, eventually earning a B.S. in Civil Engineering, an MBA, and a PhD in Psychology and Organizational Behavior.

Dr. White achieved international recognition as CEO of Blount World Trade Corporation; owner and Managing Director of ACEC Centrifugal Pumps NV, Belgium; and as Vice-President and Division Manager of Ingersoll Rand Equipment Corporation.

Throughout his career, he has bought, expanded, and sold 23 companies, operating in 44 countries. Jim acquires struggling businesses to revive and develop them into profitable enterprises using his business turnaround strategy. To date, Jim has generated more than $1.8 billion in revenue.

CPSIA information can be obtained
at www.ICGtesting.com
Printed in the USA
LVHW061228120520
655429LV00016B/346/J